Woman's Weekly

SEASONAL COOKBOOK

Woman's Weekly®

CONTENTS

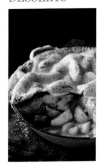

Nutritional values are per serving, or per item in the case of individual items, and are for the maximum number of servings.

STARTERS

MAIN MEALS

DESSERTS

TEATIME TREATS

SPRING

Anchovy and Red Onion Toasts

Serves 6
Calories: 140
Fat: 4g
Saturated fat: 1.5g
Suitable for freezing: ✗

- 1 ciabatta loaf
- 2 x 50g cans anchovies
- 2 tablespoons olive oil
- 1 small red onion, peeled and finely chopped
- Zest of 1 lemon
- 4 tablespoons freshly chopped parsley

1 Set the oven to 200°C or Gas Mark 6. Cut the ciabatta loaf into 12-16 slices and put them on a baking tray.

2 Drain the oil from 2 x 50g cans anchovies, into a small bowl and mix in the olive oil.

3 Brush the bread lightly on both sides with the olive oil, leaving 2 tablespoons in the bowl. Bake the slices of toast for about 10 minutes until crisp and golden – you may need to turn them once to toast on both sides.

4 Add the chopped onion, lemon zest, parsley and chopped anchovies to the reserved oil. If you prefer, you can rinse the anchovies to get rid of some of the saltiness before you chop them up.

5 Mix lightly. Spoon the anchovy mixture on top of the toasts. Arrange on a platter.

TIP

To save time you could use the topping on crispbreads or mini toasts instead of making the toasts yourself

Chinese Duck Pancakes

Serves 6

Calories: 387

Fat: 14g

Saturated fat: 4g

Suitable for freezing: ✗

- 2 duck legs and 2 duck breasts
- 2 level teaspoons Chinese Five Spice powder
- ½ level teaspoon salt
- 2 star anise
- Pared rind and juice of 1 orange
- 4 tablespoons rice wine, or sherry
- 100ml (3½fl oz) chicken stock

FOR THE PLUM SAUCE:
- 500g (1lb) red plums, halved and stoned
- 1 medium red onion, peeled and cut into thin wedges
- 5cm (2in) piece fresh root ginger, peeled and cut into slivers
- Good pinch of Chinese Five Spice powder
- 2 tablespoons caster sugar
- 1 tablespoon oil
- Soy sauce, optional

TO SERVE:
- 18-20 Chinese pancakes
- 6-8 spring onions, trimmed and cut into thin strips
- ½ cucumber, cut into thin strips

- *Baking tray lined with non-stick liner*

1 Set the oven to 160°C or Gas Mark 3. Put the duck pieces into a roasting tin. Sprinkle them with Five Spice powder and salt, add the star anise, orange parings and juice, wine or sherry, and stock. Cover with foil and cook for 2 hours until tender.

2 TO MAKE THE PLUM SAUCE: Put the plums, cut-side down, onion and ginger on the lined baking tray. Sprinkle with Five Spice powder and caster sugar, and drizzle with oil. Roast for about 1½ hours, while the duck is cooking. When it's softened, scrape everything into a food processor and whizz to a purée. Sieve. You can add some soy sauce, if you like.

3 Take the foil off the duck. Turn the oven up to 200°C or Gas Mark 6 and cook for another 20 minutes to crisp the skin on the duck – or you can put it under the grill.

4 Leave to rest for 10 minutes, then shred the meat off the bone. Serve with hot pancakes, spring onion and cucumber strips and the plum sauce.

Serves 4

Calories: 163

Fat: 1.5g

Saturated fat: 0.5g

Suitable for freezing: ✗

- 1 litre (1¼ pints) hot vegetable or chicken stock
- 1 small onion, peeled and finely chopped
- 100g (3½oz) Chantenay or baby carrots, trimmed and halved lengthways
- 1 stick celery, finely sliced
- 4 baby leeks, trimmed and chopped
- 2 cloves garlic, peeled and finely sliced
- 250g (8oz) baby new potatoes, quartered
- 100g (3½oz) fresh or frozen peas
- 3-4 heads baby pak choi or spring greens
- About 12 mint leaves, to garnish

Spring Vegetable Soup

1 Bring the stock to the boil in a large pan. Add the onion, carrots, celery, leeks and garlic. Return to the boil, then add the potatoes. Simmer for 12-15 minutes, until just tender.

2 Add the peas, then put the pak choi or spring greens on top, so it's just below the level of the stock, and simmer for another 5 minutes.

3 Spoon into warm bowls and garnish with mint, roughly chopped.

Vegetable Samosas

Makes 12

Calories: 140

Fat: 6g

Saturated fat: 3g

Suitable for freezing: ✗

- About 600g (1¼lb) roasted Mediterranean vegetables – for example, red pepper, aubergine, sweet potato and courgettes
- 1-2 tablespoons curry paste
- 6 tablespoons chopped coriander (about 30g/1oz)
- Salt and freshly ground black pepper
- 270g pack filo pastry (6 sheets)
- 60-75g (2-3oz) butter, melted
- Paprika, optional

- *1 baking sheet lined with baking parchment*

1 To make the filling, chop the veg more finely (or whizz with a stick blender), stir in the curry paste and coriander. Season well.

2 Set the oven to 200°C or Gas Mark 6. Brush 1 sheet of pastry at a time with a little butter, cut the sheet in half lengthways, then put 2 tablespoons of filling at the bottom of each strip. Fold over, and keep folding over on itself to make triangles.

3 Put them on a baking sheet lined with baking parchment and brush with butter. Repeat to use up all the pastry and filling. Sprinkle with paprika, if you like.

Queen of Heart Tarts

Makes 12

Calories: 212

Fat: 15g

Saturated fat: 7g

Suitable for freezing: ✗

- 2 x 230g sheets ready-rolled puff pastry
- 50g pack smooth mild goat's cheese, sliced into 12
- 190g jar flame-roasted peppers, drained
- 1 clove garlic, peeled and sliced
- 4 cherry tomatoes, sliced
- 1 tablespoon tiny basil leaves
- Salt and freshly ground black pepper
- 2 teaspoons olive oil
- 1 medium egg, lightly beaten

- *2 baking sheets lined with baking parchment*
- *7.5cm (3in) and 6cm (2½in) heart-shaped cutters*

1. Set the oven to 200°C or Gas Mark 6. Spread the pastry sheets out on a lightly floured surface and stamp out 12 pastry hearts with the larger cutter. Press the smaller cutter in the centre of the pastry lightly to mark a frame. Lightly score these edges.

2. Put a slice of goat's cheese on each pastry heart. Cut open the peppers flat on a chopping board. Use the smaller heart-shaped cutter to stamp out 10 shapes; fit these in the pastry hearts. Cut up the pepper trimmings and put on top of the other 2 pastry hearts.

3. Top each one with a sliver of garlic, a slice of tomato and a couple of basil leaves. Season and drizzle with the olive oil. Brush the pastry edges with egg, to glaze. Bake for 15-20 minutes, until golden brown and the bases are crisp. Serve warm or cold.

TIP

If you can't get peppers in a jar, roast 2 deseeded red peppers and remove skins

Turkey Tikka Eggs

Serves 6
Calories per egg: 393
Fat per egg: 26g
Saturated fat per egg: 5g
Suitable for freezing: ✗

- 500g (1lb) turkey mince
- 2 level tablespoon tikka curry paste
- 1 tablespoon freshly chopped coriander
- Salt and freshly ground black pepper
- 6 medium eggs, hard boiled and shelled
- 1 tablespoon plain flour
- 1 medium egg, beaten
- 60-90g (2-3½oz) dried white breadcrumbs
- Mango chutney and salad, to serve

- *Deep-frying pan with oil*

1 Heat the oil in a deep-fat fryer or chip pan to 180-190°C.

2 Mix the turkey mince with tikka paste, coriander and seasoning. Divide into 6 portions.

3 Season the flour with salt and freshly ground black pepper, then coat each egg with a light coating of the seasoned flour.

4 Tip the breadcrumbs onto a plate. Flatten out each portion of turkey mince and wrap one portion around each egg. Shape into a neat round balls. Dip the balls into the beaten egg to completely coat them, then roll them in the breadcrumbs.

5 Carefully lower 2-3 eggs into the hot oil and cook for 6-8 minutes, turning them frequently so that they colour evenly.

6 Remove the eggs from the oil and drain them on absorbent kitchen paper. Cook the remaining eggs. Serve warm or cold with mango chutney and salad.

TIP

For party eggs, you could use quails eggs and make 12-18

Squid and Village Greek Salad

Serves 4
Calories: 525
Fat: 36g
Saturated fat: 10g
Suitable for freezing: ✗

- 8 baby plum tomatoes, halved
- Salt and freshly ground black pepper
- 1 teaspoon dried oregano
- 4 tablespoons olive oil
- ½ cucumber, chopped
- ½ red onion, thinly sliced
- 10 mixed marinated Greek olives, drained
- ¼ of a white cabbage, shredded
- 200g (7oz) Greek feta cheese, cubed
- 2 tablespoons chopped fresh parsley
- Juice of 1 lemon
- Sunflower oil, for deep frying
- 4 tablespoons plain flour
- 500g (1lb) squid tubes, defrosted, if frozen, and sliced
- Lemon wedges, to serve

- *Deep fat-fryer*

1 Heat the oven to 230°C or Gas Mark 8. Put the tomatoes on a roasting tray, season with salt, sprinkle with the oregano and 2 teaspoons of the olive oil. Roast for 10 minutes.

2 Reduce the oven temperature to 150°C or Gas Mark 2, and roast for a further 20 minutes, until the tomatoes are browned around the edges but still juicy inside.

3 Put the cucumber, onion, olives, cabbage, feta cheese and parsley in a bowl. Whisk the rest of the olive oil with the lemon juice, and season to taste. Pour over the salad and stir to combine. Cover and leave to allow the flavours to mingle.

4 Meanwhile, heat the sunflower oil in a deep-fat fryer to 160°C. Put the flour on to a shallow plate and season it well. Coat the squid in the flour. Put some crumpled kitchen paper on to a tray ready to drain the squid.

5 Fry the squid in batches for a few minutes, until golden. Drain on the kitchen paper.

6 Serve the roasted tomatoes with the Greek salad, squid and lemon wedges

Serves 4

Calories: 432

Fat: 20g

Saturated fat: 6g

Suitable for freezing: ✗

FOR THE PANCAKES:
- 125g (4oz) plain flour
- Pinch of salt
- 2 medium eggs
- 300ml (½ pint) coconut milk
- 1-2 teaspoons sunflower oil, for greasing

FOR THE FILLING:
- 125g (4oz) Thai rice noodles
- 1 teaspoon caster sugar
- 2 teaspoons tamarind paste or 1 teaspoon green Thai curry paste
- 2-3 tablespoons fish sauce
- Juice of 1 lime
- 2 tablespoons vegetable oil
- 300g pack vegetable and beansprout stir-fry
- 200g (7oz) raw tiger prawns
- About 60g (2oz) roasted salted peanuts, roughly chopped
- About 4 tablespoons chopped fresh coriander leaves
- Lime wedges and sweet chilli sauce, to serve

- *20-23cm (8-9in) frying pan*

Pad Thai Pancakes

1 TO MAKE THE BATTER FOR THE PANCAKES: Sift the dry ingredients into a mixing bowl. Make a well in the centre and add the eggs and coconut milk and beat together. Alternatively, whizz with a stick blender or put into a food processor and whizz until smooth.

2 Heat the frying pan and lightly oil it. Pour in a thin stream of batter, coating the base evenly, but not too thickly. Cook over a low to medium heat, until the edges are just tinged brown and pulling away from the pan sides. Flip the pancake over and cook until golden brown.

3 Turn out onto a warmed, heatproof plate. Interleave the pancakes with greaseproof paper and keep them warm while cooking the rest of the batter. This should make about 8 pancakes.

4 Cut the noodles roughly in half, with scissors, and put them in a large bowl. Pour boiling water over them and leave to soak for 5-10 minutes.

5 Mix together the caster sugar, tamarind or Thai curry paste, the fish sauce and lime juice, to make a dressing.

6 Add 1 tablespoon of the oil to a wok or large pan and cook the vegetables for about 5 minutes, or according to pack directions. Add drained noodles and dressing, and warm through. Divide mixture between the warm pancakes.

7 Meanwhile, heat the rest of the oil in wok or pan and cook the prawns for a few minutes until they turn pink all over. Divide them between the pancakes, along with the peanuts and coriander. Roll up the pancakes and serve with lime wedges and chilli sauce.

Herb-Roasted Leg of Lamb with Crispy Mustard Dumplings and Roast Vegetables

Serves 6-8

Calories: 721

Fat: 38g

Saturated fat: 18g

Suitable for freezing: ✗

FOR THE LAMB:
- 50g can anchovies
- 16 pitted black olives
- 2 tablespoons roughly chopped fresh rosemary
- Salt and freshly ground black pepper
- 1.9-2kg (about 4lb) leg of lamb

FOR THE VEGETABLES:
- 1-1.5kg (2¼-3lb) new potatoes
- 1 bunch of carrots, trimmed and scrubbed
- 2-3 large bulbs garlic, halved
- 2 tablespoons light olive oil

FOR THE DUMPLINGS:
- 350g (12oz) self-raising flour
- 175g (6oz) shredded suet (beef or vegetarian)
- 1 large egg
- 1 tablespoon wholegrain mustard

1 Set the oven to 220°C or Gas Mark 7. Place the anchovies and their oil, black olives and rosemary in the bowl of a small food processor and whizz until blended. Or finely chop the ingredients by hand and mix together. Season.

2 Cut slashes in the top of the lamb, and fill the slashes with the olive paste. Place the lamb in a large roasting tin and cook in the centre of the oven for 30 minutes.

3 Cut the potatoes into chunks, if they are large, and put them in a bowl, along with the carrots and halved garlic bulbs. Pour the oil over and turn the vegetables to coat them.

4 Take the lamb out of the oven and reduce the oven temperature to 200°C or Gas Mark 6.

5 Arrange the vegetables around the lamb, preferably in a single layer. Return to the oven and cook for about 1 hour, turning the vegetables a couple of times so they cook evenly. The timings are for lamb that will be slightly pink (after the additional cooking with the dumplings in the tin). Allow a little longer at this stage if you like the meat to be well cooked, and less time if you like it to be quite pink.

6 TO MAKE THE DUMPLINGS: Tip the flour into a bowl and stir in the suet and seasoning. Beat the egg with the mustard and 125ml (4fl oz) cold water. Add the egg mixture to the flour and mix to a dough, adding a little more water if necessary. Divide the dough into 12 and roll each piece into a ball. Place the balls on top of the vegetables around the lamb. Return roasting tin to the oven and bake for 20-30 minutes, until the dumplings have risen and are golden.

7 Remove the tin from the oven. Transfer the contents to a warmed plate, cover loosely with foil and keep in a warm place for about 10 minutes before serving, so the meat rests.

TIP

You can use juices in the roasting tin to make gravy, if you like: pour a little boiling water into roasting tin and mix well with the juices, then strain into a separating jug or skim off fat; bring the skimmed juice to the boil and thicken with some flaked cornflour, then season to taste

Kipper Couscous

Serves 4
Calories: 377
Fat: 20g
Saturated fat: 6g
Suitable for freezing: ✗

- 1 tablespoon vegetable oil
- 200g pack frozen kipper fillets with butter, thawed
- 1 onion, peeled and diced
- 2 teaspoons curry powder or garam masala
- 175g (6oz) mixed frozen peas and green beans, thawed
- 200g (7oz) couscous
- 400ml (14fl oz) hot fish or vegetable stock
- Salt and freshly ground black pepper
- 2 medium eggs, soft boiled for 7 minutes

1 Heat the oil with the butter from the pack of the fish in a frying pan. Add the diced onion and allow it to soften over a moderate heat for 10 minutes.

2 Add the curry powder, or garam masala, the vegetables and skinned kipper flesh, broken up into chunks.

3 Sprinkle in the couscous and pour in the stock. Turn off the heat and leave to stand for 5 minutes. When the stock has been absorbed, give it a gentle stir, then season to taste.

4 Meanwhile, shell the eggs, cut them into quarters and add to the couscous. Serve warm or cold.

Serves 4
Calories: 590
Fat: 26g
Saturated fat: 14g
Suitable for freezing: ✗

- 3 good-sized sausages, skinned and broken into small chunks
- 100g (3½oz) smoked bacon bits or streaky bacon, chopped
- 1 small onion, peeled and chopped
- 1 clove garlic, peeled and crushed
- 150g (5oz) button or cup mushrooms, sliced
- 300g (10oz) dried spaghetti
- 2 medium eggs, plus 1 egg yolk, beaten
- 60g (2oz) Grana Padano cheese, grated
- Salt and freshly ground black pepper
- 2 ripe tomatoes, deseeded and chopped
- A few parsley leaves, optional

Full English Carbonara

1 Heat a frying pan, add chunks of sausage and cook for about 5 minutes, until browned. Take out of the pan and set aside.

2 Pour off all the fat from the pan. Add the bacon to the pan and fry it for a minute, then add the onion and cook for 5 minutes. Finally, add the garlic and mushrooms, cover and fry gently for a few minutes, then take the lid off and cook until all the juices have been absorbed.

3 Meanwhile, cook the pasta in boiling salted water for about 10 minutes, until just tender. Drain it, but leave a little water in the pan. Put the pasta back in the pan.

4 Beat the eggs, add the cheese with lots of seasoning and stir into the pasta quickly to coat the strands in the sauce. Add the sausage, bacon, mushroom and tomatoes. Serve at once, garnished with parsley leaves, if you like.

Leek, Red Pepper and Blue Cheese Tart

Serves 8

Calories: 323

Fat: 26g

Saturated fat: 13g

Suitable for freezing: ✗

- Knob of butter
- 1 large leek (about 300g/12oz), washed and sliced
- 2 medium eggs
- 200ml carton crème fraîche
- 21cm (8½in) shortcrust pastry tart case, baked blind
- 100g (3½oz) blue Shropshire or Stilton cheese
- 2 ready-roasted red peppers, from a jar, cut into strips
- Salad, to serve, optional

1 Set the oven to 190°C or Gas Mark 5. Melt the butter in a frying pan and add the leek and cook gently until softened.

2 Beat the eggs and crème fraîche together in a jug. Put the leeks in the pastry case on a baking sheet, and crumble in half the cheese. Pour the egg mixture into the tart case.

3 Dot the top with the rest of the cheese and add strips of pepper. Bake in the oven for 35 minutes. Serve with a salad, if you like.

Griddled Chicken, Pepper and Courgette

Serves 2

Calories: 748

Fat: 17g

Saturated fat: 3g

Suitable for freezing: ✗

- 2 small chicken breasts, skinned
- 1 lemon
- 1 teaspoon dried oregano
- 2 tablespoons olive oil
- 1 yellow or red romano pepper, halved lengthways and deseeded
- 1 fat courgette, sliced thinly lengthways into 6 slices

TO SERVE:

- 1 pack 200g (7oz) frozen microwaveable brown rice
- 2 spring onions, trimmed and chopped
- 4 ripe cherry tomatoes, chopped

1 Put a griddle pan to heat up or set the grill to high. Put the chicken breasts between 2 pieces of cling film. Bash with a rolling pin until flattened evenly. Take off top piece of cling film, sprinkle both sides of meat with grated zest from half the lemon, the oregano, 1 tablespoon of the olive oil and 1 tablespoon of lemon juice. Leave to marinate for 5 minutes or longer, while you cook the vegetables.

2 Rub some oil on the pepper halves and press them, skin-side down, on the hot griddle until beginning to char and soften. Rub the courgette strips with oil and griddle them. Set aside in a warm oven.

3 Griddle the chicken escalopes for 2-3 minutes on one side, pressing them down on the griddle, then cook for a minute on the other side.

4 Meanwhile, tip the rice into a small bowl, add the spring onions and microwave on full power for 2 minutes. Stir in the cherry tomatoes. Serve the rice with the griddled chicken and vegetables and a lemon wedge.

Saffron-Scented Fish Stew

Serves 2-3

Calories per serving: 544

Fat per serving: 51g

Saturated fat per serving: 30g

Suitable for freezing: ✗

- 300ml (1½ pints) fish stock
- 300ml carton double cream
- 1 clove garlic, peeled and crushed
- Few strands saffron
- 4 spring onions, sliced
- 350-400g (12-14oz) mixed seafood, defrosted if frozen
- Salt and freshly ground black pepper
- Garlic bread, to serve

1 Pour the fish stock into a saucepan and add the cream, garlic and saffron. Bring to the boil and boil rapidly until the mixture thickens slightly.

2 Add the spring onions and simmer for 1-2 minutes, then add the fish and simmer for about 4-5 minutes, until the fish is just cooked through, taking care not to overcook or the fish will become tough. Season with salt and freshly ground blacl pepper.

3 Spoon into serving dishes and garnish with sprigs of dill. Serve piping hot with garlic bread.

TIP

If you can't buy mixed seafood, use a selection of prawns, mussels and squid

Roast Chicken and Potato Wedges

Serves 2

Calories: 370

Fat: 7g

Saturated fat: 2g

Suitable for freezing: ✗

- 2 tablespoons olive oil
- 2 medium potatoes, unpeeled, sliced into wedges
- 2 chicken legs, skin on
- Salt and freshly ground black pepper
- Good handful of parsley sprigs
- 1 lemon, cut into 4 wedges
- ¼ small Savoy cabbage, shredded

1 Set the oven to 190°C or Gas Mark 5. Put 1 tablespoon oil in a roasting tin in the oven to heat up. Put the potato wedges in a pan, cover with water, bring to the boil and cook for 5 minutes.

2 Drain the potatoes, keeping the cooking water. Put the potatoes back in the pan to dry off, then add to the roasting tin containing the hot oil.

3 Rub a little oil all over the chicken legs and season well with salt and freshly ground black pepper. Place them on a few sprigs of parsley in another roasting tin. Add the wedges of lemon.

4 Meanwhile, chop the cabbage finely. Bring the potato cooking water to the boil and cook the cabbage for 2 minutes. Drain well, cool under cold running water. Drain again. Add to the roasting tin with chicken, stirring it in to soak up cooking juices and heat through for 5 minutes. Serve chicken on cabbage with the potato wedges. Sprinkle with parsley.

TIP

Add unpeeled garlic, onion wedges or shallots, to the roasting chicken, if you like.

Serves 4
Calories: 400
Fat: 18g
Saturated fat: 8g
Suitable for freezing: ✗

- 2 large pizza bases (300g packet)
- 4 tablespoons hot horseradish sauce
- 1 tablespoon Dijon or wholegrain mustard
- 1 large onion, peeled and thinly sliced in rings
- 8 slices pastrami (cooked, cured and spiced beef)
- 100g (3½oz) Dolcelatte cheese
- 8 small gherkins (cornichons), sliced
- Handful of rocket leaves, to serve

TIP

You could use any blue creamy cheese or mozzarella instead of Dolcelatte cheese

Pastrami and Dolcelatte Pizza

1 Set the oven to 220°C or Gas Mark 7. Spread each pizza base with horseradish sauce and mustard, then scatter with the onion.

2 Arrange halved slices of pastrami on top, and crumble the cheese over in the gaps, then scatter slices of gherkin over the cheese.

3 Put the 2 pizzas on 1 large baking sheet and bake for about 15 minutes, until the cheese has melted. Serve with some rocket leaves on top.

Tropical Pavlova

Serves 6-8
Calories: 263
Fat: 10g
Saturated fat: 6g
Suitable for freezing: ✗

- 4 large egg whites
- 250g (8oz) caster sugar
- A few drops of vanilla extract
- 1 tablespoon cornflour
- 1 tablespoon white wine vinegar

FOR THE TOPPING:
- 1 tablespoon icing sugar
- 200g carton whipped cream
- 200g carton prepared pineapple cubes
- 2 kiwi fruit, peeled and cut into wedges
- 1 x 110g carton prepared pomegranate

- *Baking sheet with non-stick liner or baking parchment*

1 Set the oven to 140°C or Gas Mark 1. Tip the egg whites into a bowl and whisk until stiff, then gradually whisk in half the sugar. Whisk in the vanilla extract. Add the rest of the sugar, cornflour and vinegar to the bowl and whisk briefly until it's all combined.

2 Turn the mixture out onto the lined baking sheet and spread it out to about a 25-30cm (10-12in) round, leaving it shallower in the centre and thicker at the edges.

3 Cook the meringue in the centre of the oven for 1-1¼ hours, or until it feels set to the touch and is an even, pale colour. Turn off the oven and leave the meringue to cool in the oven.

4 TO MAKE THE TOPPING: Just before serving, stir the icing sugar into the whipped cream and spread it over the centre of the meringue case. Top with the pineapple cubes, kiwi fruit and scatter the pomegranate seeds on top.

Orange Ricotta Pancakes

Serves 6
Calories: 297
Fat: 19g
Saturated fat: 9g
Suitable for freezing: ✗

FOR THE PANCAKES:
- 250g carton ricotta cheese
- 2 tablespoons caster sugar
- 2 large eggs, separated
- 1 orange: grated zest for batter; peeled and sliced, to serve
- 60g (2oz) plain flour
- Pinch of salt
- 2 tablespoons melted butter

TO SERVE:
- 1-2 oranges, peeled and sliced
- 2 tablespoons chopped pistachio nuts
- Clear honey, for drizzling

1 TO MAKE THE PANCAKES: Set the oven to 160°C or Gas Mark 3, for keeping the pancakes warm. Put the ricotta cheese, sugar and egg yolks in a large mixing bowl and beat well with electric beaters.

2 Add the orange zest, flour and salt, and fold in to make a smooth batter.

3 Whisk the egg whites, with clean beaters, in another bowl, to soft-peak stage, then fold into the batter mixture.

4 Warm a non-stick pan on a medium heat, then add a little of the butter. When it starts to sizzle, put 4-6 heaped tablespoons of the mixture (about 5cm/2in in diameter) into the pan and cook for 1-2 minutes on each side until slightly puffed up and golden. Keep cooked pancakes warm in oven on a baking tray.

5 Stack 3 pancakes per person on a plate, layering with orange slices. Sprinkle with chopped nuts and drizzle with honey.

TIP

You can add lemon and raisins to the mixture, instead of the orange

Makes 6
Calories: 794
Fat: 51g
Saturated fat: 28g
Suitable for freezing: ✗

FOR THE PUDDINGS:
- 125g (4oz) pitted medjool dates, chopped
- ½ level teaspoon bicarbonate of soda
- 150g (5oz) self-raising flour
- 125g (4oz) light soft brown sugar
- Pinch salt
- 90g (3oz) unsalted butter, softened
- 2 large eggs
- 5 tablespoons milk

FOR THE TOFFEE SAUCE:
- 175g (6oz) light soft brown sugar
- 60g (2oz) unsalted butter
- 300ml carton double cream
- A few drops of vanilla extract

- *6 mini pudding tins, buttered*

Medjool Date Sticky Toffee Pudding

1 TO MAKE THE PUDDINGS: Place the chopped dates in a bowl and stir in the bicarbonate of soda. Pour 150ml (¼ pint) boiling water over the dates, then leave the mixture for at least 30 minutes, so the dates can soften.

2 Set the oven to 180°C or Gas Mark 4. Tip the flour, sugar and salt into a bowl and add the butter, eggs and milk and beat until the mixture is smooth. Fold in the dates. Divide the mixture between the pudding tins, then place the tins on a baking sheet.

3 Bake the puddings in the oven for 20-25 minutes, or until they have risen and feel just firm to the touch in the centre.

4 Meanwhile, TO MAKE THE SAUCE: Melt the butter in a saucepan and stir in the sugar, then the cream. Stir the mixture over a low heat until the sugar dissolves. Increase the heat and simmer the sauce until it thickens to the desired consistency. Remove the pan from the heat.

5 Remove the puddings from the oven and leave them to cool in the tins for 2-3 minutes, then ease them out of the tins and place them on serving plates. Re-warm the sauce, if necessary, and spoon over the puddings. Any extra sauce may be served in a jug.

❋ *Pack the cold puddings in a freezer container and freeze them for up to 1 month. The sauce is not suitable for freezing*

Note: Any leftover puddings may be kept in the fridge for up to 2 days. To reheat the puddings individually, place a pudding on a plate and spoon over some of the sauce, then heat in a microwave oven for about 1 minute on full power.

Coconut Panna Cotta with Passion Fruit Sauce

Serves 4-5

Calories: 432

Fat: 38g

Saturated fat: 18g

Suitable for freezing: ✗

FOR THE PANNA COTTA:
- 3 leaves gelatine
- 300ml carton double cream
- 60g (2oz) caster sugar
- 165ml carton coconut milk
- A few drops of vanilla extract

FOR THE SAUCE:
- 4 passion fruit
- 1 tablespoon rum
- 2-3 tablespoons clear honey

- **4-5 small moulds or coffee cups**

1 TO MAKE THE PANNA COTTA: Place the gelatine leaves in a small bowl and pour some cold water over them to cover them (the amount of water is not important as long as the gelatine is covered). Leave the gelatine to sponge for a few minutes.

2 Meanwhile, pour the double cream into a saucepan and bring it to the boil. Remove the pan from the heat, add the caster sugar and stir until the sugar dissolves.

3 Lift the gelatine out of the water and squeeze out any excess moisture, then add it to the hot cream, and stir untnil it dissolves. Stir in the coconut milk and vanilla extract, to taste. Pour the mixture into small moulds or coffee cups and place in the fridge to set, preferably overnight.

4 TO MAKE THE SAUCE: Halve the passion fruit and scoop the seeds out into a bowl and discard the shells. Stir in the rum, then sufficient rum, to taste.

5 To serve, dip the moulds briefly in hot water, and gently ease the edges of the panna cotta, then turn them out onto plates. Serve the sauce in a small bowl or spooned over the panna cotta.

Tangy Lime Meringue Roulade

Serves 6-8
Calories: 260
Fat: 15g
Saturated fat: 9.5g
Suitable for freezing: ✗

FOR THE MERINGUE:
- 5 egg whites
- 150g (5oz) caster sugar
- 1 level tablespoon cornflour

FOR THE FILLING:
- 300ml carton whipping cream
- 6 tablespoons lime marmalade, sieved
- Zest and 2 tablespoons juice of 1 lime
- Icing sugar, for dusting

- *23 x 33cm (9 x 13in) Swiss roll tin, lined*

1 Set the oven to 150°C or Gas Mark 2.
TO MAKE THE MERINGUE: Whisk the egg whites until stiff, then gradually whisk in half the caster sugar until the entire mixture is stiff. Add the remaining sugar and cornflour and whisk briefly until it's all mixed in.

2 Spoon the meringue into the lined tin and level the surface, taking care not to press out too much of the air. Bake it in the centre of the oven for about 45 minutes, until it's a pale golden colour and just firm to the touch.

3 Remove the baked meringue from the oven and leave it to cool, uncovered.

4 TO MAKE THE FILLING: Whisk the whipping cream until it just forms soft peaks. Stir in the marmalade, lime zest and juice.

5 Turn the meringue out on to a sheet of baking parchment that has been dusted with icing sugar and peel away the lining paper.

6 Spread the cream filling over the roulade and use the baking parchment to help roll it up. Dust over a little extra icing sugar before serving.

Serves: 8-12
Calories: 493
Fat: 33g
Saturated fat: 20g
Suitable for freezing: ✗

FOR THE BASE:
- 12 digestive biscuits, crushed
- 60g (2oz) unsalted butter, melted

FOR THE CARAMEL:
- 100g (3½oz) caster sugar
- 2 level tablespoons liquid glucose
- 300ml carton whipping cream
- Large pinch of salt flakes – Maldon

FOR THE CHOCOLATE LAYER:
- 2 medium egg whites
- 125g (4oz) caster sugar
- 300ml carton whipping cream
- A few drops of vanilla extract
- 300g (10oz) dark chocolate, melted
- Pinch of salt flakes, to decorate

- *20cm (8in) loose-bottomed cake tin, base-lined with baking parchment*
- *Small disposable piping bag*

Salted Caramel Chocolate Torte

1 TO MAKE THE BASE: Mix the crushed biscuits with the melted butter. Tip the mixture into the base of the lined cake tin and press it down well. Chill the biscuit mixture while making the caramel.

2 TO MAKE THE CARAMEL: Pour 4 tablespoons water into a pan and add the sugar and liquid glucose. Place the pan over a low heat and stir until the sugar dissolves. Wash down any crystals from around the sides of the pan, using a damp pastry brush. Increase the heat and boil the syrup until it turns golden. While the syrup is boiling, bring the cream to the boil in a separate pan or in a jug in a microwave oven. Remove the syrup pan from the heat and carefully pour in the hot cream, taking care in case the mixture splatters. Stir well, then return the pan to the heat and simmer for 2-3 minutes. Remove the pan from the heat and leave mixture to cool and thicken.

3 Stir the salt into the caramel. Pour most of the caramel over the biscuit base and spread it out almost to the edges. Reserve the remaining caramel for the topping. Chill while making the chocolate layer.

4 TO MAKE THE CHOCOLATE LAYER: Place the egg whites and sugar in a bowl over a pan of hot water. Stir until the sugar has completely dissolved, and the liquid feels smooth to your fingers. Remove the bowl from above the hot water, then whisk the mixture to form a thick meringue.

5 Whisk the cream and vanilla extract until it just forms soft peaks. Fold the melted chocolate into the meringue mixture, and then fold in the cream. Pour the mixture over the caramel and smooth the top. Chill the torte until set.

6 Spoon the reserved caramel into the piping bag and cut off the end of the bag to give a small hole. Pipe squiggles of caramel over the top of the torte. To serve, remove torte from the tin, peel away the baking parchment from the sides and remove it from the base. Sprinkle some flakes of salt over the top.

Slow-roasted Rhubarb

Serves 6-8
Calories: 134
Fat: 0g
Saturated fat: 0g
Suitable for freezing: ✔

- 800g-1kg (1lb 10oz-2lb) rhubarb
- 250g (8oz) caster sugar
- Zested rind and juice of 2 oranges
- Ice cream, to serve

1 Set the oven to 120°C or Gas Mark ½. Cut the rhubarb into 6-8cm (2½-3¼in) lengths and place them in a non-metallic ovenproof dish, sprinkle over the caster sugar and orange zest, and stir to coat the rhubarb in the sugar. Pour over the orange juice. Cover the dish with a lid (see Tip, below).

2 Cook the rhubarb in the centre of the oven for 1-1½ hours, or until the rhubarb is just tender.

3 Remove rhubarb from the oven and leave it to cool. Serve at room temperature or chilled, with ice cream. The rhubarb will keep for up to 3-4 days in the fridge.

❋ *The rhubarb can be packed into a plastic container and frozen for up to 1 month. Let it defrost thoroughly before serving*

TIP

If the dish doesn't have a lid, cover with a sheet of baking parchment with foil over the top of that

Serves 4-5
Calories: 331
Fat: 10g
Saturated fat: 4g
Suitable for freezing: ✗

- 125g (4oz) caster sugar, plus extra for coating soufflé dish
- 4 large eggs, separated
- 50g (1¾oz) plain flour
- 250ml (8fl oz) milk
- 4 tablespoons Grand Marnier
- Zested rind and juice of 2 oranges
- Icing sugar, for dusting

- *1.25 litre (2 pint) soufflé dish, buttered*

TIP

This recipe also works with Cointreau instead of Grand Marnier

Orange and Grand Marnier Soufflé

1 Set the oven to 220°C or Gas Mark 7. Sprinkle some of the extra sugar in the soufflé dish and turn the dish to coat the inside with the sugar and tip out the excess.

2 Whisk half the sugar with the egg yolks until the mixture thickens and is pale in colour. Sift over the flour, then fold it in with a metal spoon.

3 Bring the milk to the boil and pour it over the egg yolk mixture, stirring well. Return the mixture to the pan and cook it over a low heat, stirring well until it's thickened into a smooth sauce. Remove the pan from the heat and stir in the Grand Marnier and orange juice and rind. Press a sheet of cling film against the surface of the sauce to prevent a skin forming on it, and leave to cool.

5 Whisk the egg whites until stiff, then gradually whisk in the rest of the sugar. Fold the egg whites into the sauce and pour into the soufflé dish.

6 Bake in the centre of the oven for 15-20 minutes, or until it's well risen and it is slightly wobbly. Remove the soufflé from the oven, dust with icing sugar and serve immediately.

Coffee and Walnut Traybake

Cuts into 15 squares

Calories: 411

Fat: 26g

Saturated fat: 18g

Suitable for freezing: ✔

FOR THE TRAYBAKE:

- 100g packet walnuts
- 1 tablespoon instant coffee granules
- 3 tablespoons boiling water
- 200g (7oz) unsalted butter, softened
- 200g (7oz) light soft brown sugar
- 200g (7oz) self-raising flour
- 4 medium eggs

FOR THE TOPPING:

- 1 tablespoon instant coffee granules
- 2 tablespoons boiling water
- 250g (8oz) icing sugar
- 125g (4oz) unsalted butter
- 15 walnut halves

- 18 x 28cm (7 x 11in) oblong tin, lined with baking parchment
- Large piping bag fitted with large star piping tube

1 Set the oven to 180°C or Gas Mark 4.
TO MAKE THE TRAYBAKE: Whizz the walnuts in a food processor or blender until they are finely ground. Tip the instant coffee into a mixing bowl and add the boiling water and stir until the coffee has dissolved. Add the butter, sugar, flour, eggs and ground walnuts to the bowl, then beat the mixture well until it is smooth. Spoon the mixture into the lined tin and level the surface.

2 Bake the cake in the centre of the oven for about 40-50 minutes, or until it is just firm to the touch in the centre. Remove the cake from the oven and leave it to cool in the tin for a few minutes, then transfer to a wire rack to cool completely.

3 TO MAKE THE COFFEE BUTTERCREAM TOPPING: Tip the instant coffee into a mixing bowl and add the boiling water and stir until the coffee dissolves. Add the icing sugar and butter to the bowl and beat the mixture until it is smooth. Fill the piping bag with the mixture.

4 Cut the cake into 15 squares, then pipe a swirl of buttercream on the top of each square, and press a walnut half on the top of each.

❋ *The undecorated traybake may be wrapped whole in a freezer bag and then frozen for up to 1 month. Allow the cake to defrost before cutting it into squares and decorating with the topping*

Crumpets

Makes about 18

Calories: 94

Fat: 3g

Saturated fat: 1g

Suitable for freezing: ✔

- 350g (12oz) strong plain flour
- 1 level teaspoon salt
- 7g sachet fast action dried yeast
- 300ml (½ pint) milk
- Sunflower oil, for frying and greasing

- 6 x 7cm (2¾in) cooking rings or crumpet rings

1 Tip the flour into a bowl and stir in the salt and yeast. Pour 300ml (½ pint) boiling water over the milk and check the temperature of the mixture; it should be just lukewarm. If it's too hot, let it cool slightly; if it's not warm enough, then warm it slightly in a microwave oven or saucepan, but take care not to get it too hot.

2 Add the warm liquid to the flour, then beat it well for about 5 minutes, either with a wooden spoon, or using the paddle beater of a table-top food mixer. The mixture should be quite liquid and of a spoonable consistency.

3 Grease the cooking or crumpet rings with sunflower oil and smear a light covering of oil over the base of a solid frying pan. Place the rings on the base of the pan and heat. When both the pan and rings are hot, spoon in the batter to about half fill the rings. Cook the mixture over a gentle to moderate heat for about 8-10 minutes, then remove the rings and turn the crumpets over. Cook the crumpets for 2-3 minutes until lightly golden.

4 Remove the crumpets from the pan and keep them warm until they are all cooked. Serve the crumpets hot with melted butter.

✳ *Pack the crumpets into freezer bags, seal and freeze for up to 1 month. Allow the crumpets to defrost before toasting them*

TIP

The crumpets may be left to cool, then toasted to heat them

Makes 12
Calories: 226
Fat: 10g
Saturated fat:
Suitable for freezing: ✗

FOR THE CAKES:
- 125g (4oz) butter, softened
- 125g (4oz) caster sugar
- 125g (4oz) self-raising flour
- 2 large eggs
- Finely grated rind 1 lemon, plus 2 tablespoons juice

FOR THE TOPPING:
- 175g (6oz) icing sugar
- 2-4 tablespoons lemon juice
- Yellow liquid food colouring
- Hundreds and Thousands

- *12-hole bun tray, lined with paper cases*

TIP

To make simple flower decorations, roll out some yellow sugarpaste thinly and cut into long strips. Fold each strip in half widthways, and gather up, with the joined ends underneath, to give a flower shape. Cut off any excess sugarpaste. Place on the cakes when the icing is still wet so that they stick in place

Tangy Lemon Cupcakes

1 Set the oven to 190°C or Gas Mark 5. Beat together the butter and caster sugar in a bowl until well combined, then add the flour, eggs and lemon rind and juice to the bowl. Beat the mixture until smooth, then divide it between the paper cases in the bun tray.

2 Bake the cakes in the centre of the oven for 15-18 minutes, until they have risen, are a light even colour and are just firm to the touch in the centre.

3 Remove the cakes from the oven and transfer to a wire rack to cool completely.

4 TO MAKE THE TOPPING: Sift the icing sugar into a bowl, then add enough lemon juice to give an icing, which is thick enough that it will cover the top of the cakes, but runny enough that it will flow to give a smooth surface. Beat in a few drops of yellow food colouring to give the desired shade of icing.

5 Spoon the icing onto the top of the cakes, spreading it out almost to the edges of the cakes using a palette knife and sprinkle over Hundreds and Thousands before the icing has set. Leave for the icing to set before serving.

Madeleines

Makes 18-20
Calories: 53
Fat: 3g
Saturated fat: 2g
Suitable for freezing: ✔

- 2 medium eggs
- 60g (2oz) caster sugar
- Zest 1 lemon
- 60g (2oz) plain flour
- ½ level teaspoon baking powder
- 60g (2oz) butter, melted
- Icing sugar, for dusting

- *Madeleine tins, buttered and floured (see Tip)*

1 Set the oven to 200°C or Gas Mark 6. Tip the eggs into a bowl and add the caster sugar, then whisk until the mixture is light and frothy and a trail is left when the whisk is lifted out of the mixture. Whisk in the lemon rind.

2 Sift the flour and baking powder over the surface of the egg and sugar mixture and pour the butter around the edge of the bowl. Carefully fold all the ingredients together. Divide the mixture between the madeleine tins.

3 Bake the madeleines, towards the top of the oven, for 12-15 minutes, or until they have risen and are light golden in colour and they spring back when lightly pressed.

4 Remove the tins from the oven and leave the madeleines to cool for a few minutes, then carefully ease them out of the tin and transfer to a wire rack to cool completely. Dust icing sugar over the top before serving.

✳ *Once cooled, pack the madeleines into a freezer container, seal and freezer for up to 1 month. Allow the madeleines to defrost, then dust with icing sugar before serving*

TIP

Use silicone madeleine moulds, which are flexible, so it's easy to remove the sponge cakes. Just place the mould on a baking sheet to support it during cooking

Serves 11

Calories: 867

Fat: 38g

Saturated fat: 18

Suitable for freezing: ✔

- 250g (8oz) butter, softened
- 250g (8oz) caster sugar
- 4 medium eggs
- 300g (10oz) plain flour
- 2 tablespoons milk
- 1 level teaspoon mixed spice
- 500g (1lb) dried mixed fruit
- 250g packet dried apricots, chopped
- 200g carton glace cherries
- 100g packet ground almonds
- 500g packet white marzipan
- 4-5 level tablespoons apricot glaze or sieved apricot jam

- *20cm (8in) round cake tin, lined with baking parchment*
- *Ribbon, optional*

Simnel Cake

1 Set the oven to 150°C or Gas Mark 2. Cream together the butter and sugar until the mixture is light and fluffy. Beat in the eggs, one at a time, adding a dessertspoon of the flour along with each egg to help prevent the mixture from curdling. Beat in the milk and mixed spice, then fold in the remaining flour, dried fruit, apricots, cherries and ground almonds.

2 Spoon ½ the fruit cake mixture into the lined tin. Roll out ¼ marzipan to a circle slightly smaller than the cake tin. Place the marzipan circle on top of the mixture in the cake tin, then spoon the rest of the cake mixture on top. Level the top of the cake with a wet hand to give a smooth surface.

3 Place the cake in the oven, on the shelf just below the centre of the oven so that the cake is central in the oven. Bake the cake for 3-3½hours, or until the cake feels just firm to the touch in the centre. If the top of the cake starts to brown too quickly, then cover it with a sheet of baking parchment.

4 Remove the cake from the oven and place the tin on a wire rack, so that air can circulate around the tin. Leave the cake to cool in the tin.

5 Remove the cake from the tin and peel away the lining paper. Warm the apricot glaze or jam until it's runny, then brush a thin layer over the top of the cake. Take about a third of the remaining marzipan and roll it out to a circle just larger than the cake. Place the cake tin on top, then cut around the tin to neaten the circle. Place the circle of marzipan on the top of the cake. Use a sharp knife to mark a criss-cross pattern on the marzipan. Place the cake under a hot grill until the marzipan starts to turn golden.

6 Knead together the remaining marzipan and the trimmings from cutting out the circle and divide into 11 and roll each piece into a smooth ball. Place the balls evenly around the top of the cake, pressing them down gently so they stick to the cake, but without squashing them too much.

7 Return the cake to under the grill until the top of the marzipan balls turn golden. Remove the cake from the grill. Re-warm the glaze or jam, if necessary, and brush over the top of the marzipan.

8 If liked, a ribbon may be tied around the cake for serving, but either use a moisture-resistant ribbon, or don't leave it on the cake for too long as the fat in the cake may cause the ribbon to discolour.

✸ *The cake without the marzipan topping may be frozen. Allow the cake to defrost, then decorate with marzipan*

STARTERS

MAIN MEALS

DESSERTS

TEATIME TREATS

SUMMER

Easy Borscht with Goat's Cheese Tartlets

Serves 6

Calories: 507

Fat: 34g

Saturated fat: 18g

Suitable for freezing: ✔

- 2 tablespoons sunflower oil
- 60g (2oz) butter
- 1 onion, peeled and diced
- 1 large carrot, peeled and diced
- 1 medium potato, peeled and diced
- 2 cloves garlic, peeled and crushed
- 500g (1lb) raw beetroot, peeled and diced
- 1 tablespoon caster sugar
- 900ml (1½ pints) hot home-made chicken or vegetable stock
- 2 tablespoons crème fraîche
- A few sprigs of dill

FOR THE TARTLETS:

Makes 12

- 375g packet ready-rolled puff pastry
- 130-150g log of goat's cheese, with rind on
- A few sprigs of thyme
- Salt and freshly ground black pepper

- *Baking sheet, lined with non-stick liner or baking parchment*

1 Put the oil and butter in a large pan over a low heat. Add the onion, carrot, potato and garlic, and cook for about 15 minutes until softened.

2 Add the beetroot and caster sugar and cook for 3-4 minutes. Pour in the stock, bring to the boil and simmer for an hour.

3 Meanwhile, TO MAKE THE TARTLETS: Set the oven to 200°C or Gas Mark 6. Unroll the pastry. Cut out 12 x 6.5cm (2¾in) rounds. Mark a thin border around each one using a 5cm (2in) cutter. Put on the lined baking sheet, prick the middles a few times with a fork. Bake for 10 minutes above the centre of the oven. Cut the goat's cheese into 12 slices. Push down the centres of the tartlets and press a slice of cheese inside each one. Add thyme sprigs and season. Bake for 10 minutes more.

4 Whizz soup in a food processor, then push the purée through a sieve Reheat; add more stock or water to thin, if you like. Ladle into warm bowls; top with crème fraîche and dill fronds. Serve with tartlets.

❊ *Soup may be frozen for up to 1 month. Allow to defrost before reheating thoroughly. Tartlets not suitable for freezing*

TIP

If you don't have time to make tartlets, serve with garlic bread

Griddled Halloumi, Courgette and Asparagus

Serves 4

Calories: 306

Fat: 26g

Saturated fat: 11g

Suitable for freezing: ✗

- 200g (7oz) asparagus spears
- 6 baby courgettes, halved lengthways
- 2 tablespoons olive oil
- 225g packet of halloumi cheese, sliced into 12
- 4 handfuls of pea shoots or baby salad leaves

FOR THE DRESSING:
- 2 tablespoons olive oil
- Juice of ½ a lemon
- ½ teaspoon each soy sauce and honey
- 2 teaspoons caraway seeds, toasted

1 Coat the asparagus spears and courgette lightly in olive oil and cook in batches in a griddle pan until tender. Set aside on a warm plate. Coat the cheese slices in the remaining oil and griddle them.

2 Whisk all the dressing ingredients in a jug. Arrange the cheese and the vegetables on warm plates. Drizzle with the dressing and put a few pea shoots or salad leaves on top.

TIP

You can replace halloumi with crumbled feta, and caraway with fennel seeds

Makes 16 slices

Calories: 190

Fat: 14g

Saturated fat: 6.5g

Suitable for freezing: ✗

- 3 cloves garlic
- 6-8 ripe tomatoes
- Small bunch of basil
- 6 tablespoons good olive oil
- Salt and freshly ground black pepper
- 8 slices ciabatta bread
- A handful of rocket leaves
- Balsamic vinegar, optional

Tomato and Rocket Bruschetta

1 Peel and crush 2 of the garlic cloves and put in a bowl. Quarter, deseed and roughly chop the tomatoes, and add to the bowl with the torn basil, 4 tablespoons of the olive oil, and seasoning.

2 Heat a griddle pan or the grill. Brush the ciabatta bread on both sides with the rest of the olive oil.

3 Griddle or grill the bread on both sides. Halve the last garlic clove and rub the cut sides over the toasted bread.

4 Pile the tomato mixture on the toasts, and garnish with a few rocket leaves. Drizzle with a little more oil, and vinegar, if you like.

Salmon Rillettes

Serves 6

Calories: 307

Fat: 28g

Saturated fat: 13g

Suitable for freezing: ✗

- 100g (3½oz) unsalted butter, softened
- 4 tablespoons crème fraîche
- 4 tablespoons mayonnaise
- Finely zested rind and juice of 1 lemon
- 2 x 160g packets hot smoked salmon fillets, skinned
- 2 level tablespoons capers, rinsed and drained
- 2 level tablespoons chopped fresh dill
- Salt and freshly ground black pepper
- Oatcakes, sprigs of dill, salmon caviar and lemon wedges, to serve

1 Beat the butter well, then beat in the crème fraîche, mayonnaise, lemon rind and zest.

2 Break the salmon into flakes and add to the mixture. Use a fork to mash the salmon into the mixture, leaving it a little coarse. Stir in the capers and dill, and season to taste with salt and freshly ground black pepper.

3 Keep the mixture chilled until serving. Serve with oatcakes, and garnished with sprigs of dill, a little salmon caviar and lemon wedges.

TIP

Don't mash the salmon too much, as it's better to have a bit of texture in the mixture

Spanish-style Prawns

Serves 2-3

Calories: 171

Fat: 8g

Saturated fat: 1g

Suitable for freezing: ✗

- 2 tablespoons olive oil
- 1-2 cloves garlic, peeled and finely sliced
- 1 fennel bulb, sliced thinly
- A handful of flat-leaf parsley sprigs
- 500g (1lb) cherry tomatoes on the vine (Piccolini)
- 5 tablespoons manzanilla sherry
- 1 tablespoon sun-dried tomato paste
- 10-15 large raw prawns, peeled, leaving tail shell on
- Salt and freshly ground black pepper
- Chunks of bread, to serve

1 Heat the olive oil in a large, shallow pan. Add the garlic, fennel and parsley stalks and fry gently for 12-15 minutes, until tender. Add the cherry tomatoes, sherry and tomato paste. Bring to the boil, then simmer gently for 25 minutes, until thickened.

2 Push the prawns into the sauce, cook for 2 minutes. Turn them and cook for 1-2 minutes, or until they're pink all over. Season and sprinkle with parsley leaves to serve. Serve with chunks of bread.

Courgette Fritters with Tomato and Avocado Salad

Serves 3-6 (6 fritters)

Calories: 157

Fat: 11g

Saturated fat per: 2.8g

Suitable for freezing: ✗

- 5 tablespoons (60g/2oz) self-raising flour
- Salt and freshly ground black pepper
- 1 large egg
- 1 large courgette (175g/6oz), coarsely grated
- 2 spring onions, trimmed and chopped
- 2 heaped tablespoons (60g/2oz) ricotta cheese
- 2 tablespoons olive oil

FOR THE SALAD:

- 2 ripe tomatoes, chopped
- 1 ripe avocado, peeled, stoned and chopped
- 1 spring onion, trimmed and chopped
- A few basil leaves
- A little olive oil

1 Put the flour in a large bowl, season, beat in the egg, then stir in the courgette and onions. Lightly fold in the ricotta cheese, leaving it a bit lumpy.

2 Heat the olive oil in a large frying pan and add 6 spoonfuls of the batter mixture (or cook 3 at a time in half the oil). Cook for 2 minutes on each side, over a medium heat, until golden.

3 TO MAKE THE SALAD: Mix the salad ingredients together, tearing in the basil leaves, then adding a dash of olive oil. Serve at once.

Bloody Mary Sorbet

Makes 1 litre (1¾ pints)

Serves 10

Calories: 100

Fat: 0.3g

Saturated fat: 0.1g

Suitable for freezing: ✔

- 150g (5oz) granulated sugar
- 1 shallot, peeled
- 1 cucumber, peeled and deseeded
- 1 large red pepper, deseeded
- 500g (1lb) ripe red plum tomatoes, quartered
- 5 tablespoons vodka
- 5 tablespoons lemon juice
- 5 tablespoons tomato purée
- 1 teaspoon each Tabasco and Worcestershire sauces
- Salt and freshly ground black pepper
- Celery stalks and lime wedges, to serve
- Cheesy biscuits, to serve, optional

1 Put the sugar and 150ml (5fl oz) water in a small pan, simmer for a few minutes until the sugar dissolves. Boil the syrup for 4 minutes to thicken it. Leave to cool for 10 minutes.

2 Roughly chop the shallot, cucumber and pepper, put into a blender, or food processor, and whizz to chop it finely. Add the tomatoes, whizz again. Push the mixture through a coarse sieve into a large bowl or jug. Add the sugar syrup and the rest of the ingredients, to taste. Mix well, then push through a fine sieve.

3 Churn the sorbet in an ice-cream maker. Or pour it into a freezer container. Freeze for 6-8 hours. Soften for about 30 minutes, put in a food processor and whizz until just smooth. Freeze again in an ice-cream container for at least 42 hours, to firm.

4 Take out of the freezer and put in the fridge for 10 minutes before serving.

5 Spoon into chilled glasses. Serve with celery stalks and lime wedges, and some thin, cheesy biscuits, if you like.

TIPS

If you forget to whizz the frozen mixture, don't worry — serve it as an icy granita

Serve as a starter, between courses or as a dessert!

Serves 4

Calories: 51

Fat: 2g

Saturated fat: 0.5g

Suitable for freezing: ✗

- 100g (3½oz) fresh or frozen broadbeans
- 100g (3½oz) fresh or frozen peas
- 2 spring onions, trimmed and chopped
- 1 tablespoon frozen Thai herb mix
- 1-2 teaspoons sesame oil
- Dash of Thai fish or soy sauce
- Good squeeze of lime juice, optional
- Handful of fresh coriander (or mint) leaves, optional

TO SERVE:
- Young carrots, radishes, cauliflower florets, and pepper strips
- Pitta bread, toasted

Quick Thai Green Dip

1 Bring 200ml (7fl oz) water to the boil in a pan. Add the beans, peas, spring onions and herbs, half cover with a lid and simmer for 5-8 minutes, until tender. With a stick blender, purée the vegetables, herbs and liquid in the pan, adding the oil and fish or soy sauce, plus lime juice and coriander or mint, if using, to taste.

2 Serve with the fresh vegetables and toasted pitta bread for dipping.

Serves 6

Calories: 270

Fat: 15g

Saturated fat: 7g

Suitable for freezing: ✗

- 3 x 450-500g (15oz-1lb) poussin,
- 6 tablespoons olive oil
- 2 tablespoons mixed herbs – rosemary, thyme, sage, parsley – very finely chopped
- 2 lemons, finely sliced
- Salt and freshly ground black pepper
- 1 large red chilli, deseeded and finely sliced

Spatchcock Poussin with Lemon and Chilli Sauce

1 TO SPATCHCOCK THE POUSSIN: Put the bird, breast down, on a chopping board and cut up both sides of the backbone and remove it. Use strong scissors if you don't have poultry shears.

2 Flatten the bird out and put in 2 skewers crosswise to keep the legs and wings flattened while it cooks. Put the poussin in a large dish and coat with the olive oil and sprinkle well with herbs. Season with salt and freshly ground black pepper and add the lemon slices. Cover and leave for about an hour or longer.

3 Set the oven to 200°C or Gas Mark 6. Put a shallow-ish roasting tin in to heat up. Put the poussin in the tin. Set aside the lemon slices. Cook

the poussin in the oven for 30-35 minutes, until just browned and a skewer, when inserted into the thigh, releases clear juices.

4 Remove from the tin and leave them covered in foil. Put the lemon slices on the tray and put back in the oven at 220°C or Gas Mark 7 and cook for 15-20 minutes, until just caramelised.

5 Meanwhile, pour the juices into a wide pan, bring to the boil, add the chilli and reduce to a sauce for about 10 minutes, while the lemon slices cook. Season to taste.

6 Chop each spatchcock in half and arrange in a bowl or on a platter. Scatter with the lemon slices and pour the hot dressing over.

No-cook Thai Beef Salad

Serves 2-3

Calories: 315

Fat: 11g

Saturated fat: 2g

Suitable for freezing: ✗

- 125g (4oz) bundle rice noodles
- About 100g (3½oz) cold cooked rare roast beef, thinly sliced into strips
- 1 long red chilli, deseeded and cut into long thin strips
- 150g (5oz) beansprouts
- A good handful (about 10g/¼oz) each of fresh coriander and basil leaves, plus some mint leaves
- 2 teaspoons roasted peanuts, roughly crushed
- Sweet chilli sauce, to serve

FOR THE DRESSING:
- Juice of 1 lime
- 2 tablespoons vegetable oil
- 2 tablespoons Thai fish sauce

1 Put the rice noodles in a large bowl. Pour boiling water over them and leave for 4 minutes, until softened. Drain well, rinse under cold water and put back into the bowl.

2 TO MAKE THE DRESSING: Mix in the lime juice, vegetable oil and Thai fish sauce in another large bowl. Mix about half of this dressing into the noodles and divide them between 2 or 3 plates. Toss the beef slices in the remaining dressing. With tongs, arrange them on the noodles.

3 To the dressing that's left, add the chilli, beansprouts, coriander, basil and mint leaves. Pile this on top of the beef and noodles. Sprinkle with crushed peanuts. Serve with sweet chilli sauce.

TIP

Leftover chicken, lamb or pork would work just as well in this recipe. If you don't have fresh beansprouts, use Little Gem or spinach leaves

Serves 2

Calories: 405

Fat: 22g

Saturated fat: 11g

Suitable for freezing: ✗

- 250g minced lamb
- 50g white breadcrumbs
- 1 clove garlic, peeled and crushed
- Dash Tabasco sauce
- 1 level teaspoon ground coriander
- 1 level teaspoon ground cumin
- Salt and freshly ground black pepper
- 4 mini pitta bread, to serve

FOR THE DRESSING:
- ½ x 200g carton Greek yogurt
- ¼ cucumber

TIP

It's often cheaper to buy frozen lamb, rather than fresh lamb, and as it's usually "free flow", it's easy to weigh out the quantity that's needed

Lamb Kebabs

1 Place the minced lamb in a bowl and add the other ingredients and mix well. Divide the mixture into 12 and shape each into a ball. Thread the balls onto skewers. Cook the lamb balls under a hot grill and cook for 10-15 minutes, turning them occasionally so they cook through.

2 TO MAKE THE DRESSING: Tip the yogurt into a bowl and stir in the cucumber and seasoning.

3 Warm the pitta bread before serving. Serve the lamb either still on the skewers with the pitta and dressing, or slit open the pitta bread and fill each with 3 lamb balls and spoon on some of the dressing.

Mediterranean Aubergines

Serves 4

Calories: 180

Fat: 13.5g

Saturated fat: 3.5g

Suitable for freezing: ✗

- 1 onion, peeled and chopped
- 3 tablespoons olive oil
- 1-2 cloves garlic
- 400g can chopped tomatoes
- 1 tablespoon tomato ketchup
- Salt and freshly ground black pepper
- 2 good-sized aubergines
- 60g (2oz) stoned olives, drained and chopped
- 60g (2oz) ready-grated mozzarella
- About 10 basil leaves, shredded

- *Baking sheet*
- *Shallow ovenproof dish*

1 Fry the onion for a few minutes in 1 tablespoon of the olive oil. Add the garlic and cook for 5 minutes. Stir in the tomatoes and ketchup and simmer, uncovered, for 10-15 minutes until thickened. Season.

2 Cut each aubergine into 8 thin slices. Pick out the largest 12 slices; brush these on both sides with oil, and griddle or grill in batches until browned.

3 Set aside on a baking sheet. Griddle or grill the rest, then chop them and put in a bowl. Add 4 tablespoons tomato sauce and the olives to the chopped aubergine; mix well. Spoon just over half of the rest of the tomato sauce into the dish.

4 Set the oven to 200°C or Gas Mark 6. Lay the aubergine slices out on a board and divide the filling between them. Sprinkle with half of the cheese and half of the basil leaves. Roll each slice up. Pack them in the dish, seam-side down. Spoon the rest of the sauce over and sprinkle on the cheese.

5 Bake for 20 minutes. Sprinkle shredded basil leaves on top.

TIP

For extra speed, you could use a jar of ready-made pasta sauce and even ready-grilled aubergines

Serves 4

Calories: 285

Fat: 24g

Saturated fat : 15g

Suitable for freezing: ✗

- 1 bag washed rocket leaves
- 1 mango, peeled, stoned and sliced
- 150-175g (4-6oz) Stilton cheese, cubed

FOR THE DRESSING:
- 4 tablespoons raspberry vinegar
- 4 tablespoons olive oil
- 1 level teaspoon Dijon mustard
- Salt and freshly ground black pepper
- 125-150g (4-5oz) raspberries

Raspberry, Mango and Stilton Salad

1 Divide the rocket leaves between the serving plates and arrange the mango and Stilton on top.

2 TO MAKE THE DRESSING: Whisk together the raspberry vinegar, olive oil, mustard and seasoning, then stir in the raspberries, taking care that they don't break down too much. Spoon the dressing over the leaves and serve immediately.

Salmon and Prawn Pie

Serves 6

Calories: 483

Fat: 43g

Saturated fat: 24g

Suitable for freezing: ✗

- 3 sheets filo pastry
- 30-45g (1-1½oz) butter, melted

FOR THE FILLING:
- 350g (12oz) salmon fillet, cubed
- 200ml carton crème fraîche
- 200g carton cream cheese
- 2 medium eggs
- 2-3 tablespoons freshly chopped dill or 1-2 tablespoons freshly chopped tarragon
- 125g (4oz) large prawns
- Salt and freshly ground black pepper

- *Baking sheet*
- *20cm round loose-bottomed flan tin, buttered*

1 Set the oven to 200°C or Gas Mark 6.
TO MAKE THE FILLING: Bring a pan of water to the boil and add the salmon cubes, bring back to the boil then immediately remove the pan from the heat. Leave the salmon to poach for 2-3 minutes, until it's just cooked, then drain it well and leave it to cool.

2 Beat together the crème fraîche, cream cheese, eggs, dill or tarragon and seasoning.

3 Cut 2 sheets of filo pastry in half to give 2 square shapes. Brush 1 square of filo pastry with butter and then lay another square on top, rotating it slightly so that the points don't line up, then repeat with a 3rd square, and then the final square. Use the 4 layers of pastry to line the flan tin, pressing it well into the corners. Place the salmon and prawns into the pastry case, then pour over the cream cheese mixture. Bring the pastry over to cover the filling around the edges, leaving the pastry slightly scrunched up.

4 Brush the remaining sheet of pastry with butter, then tear them into strips and "scrunch" them up over the filling. Place the tin on the heated baking sheet and then bake in the centre of the oven for 25-30 minutes, or until the pastry is crisp and golden.

5 Remove from the oven and leave the pie to cool in the tin for about 10 minutes, for the filling to set, then lift it out of the tin and leave it to cool, still on the base, as this makes it easier to move. The pie may be served warm or at room temperature, with green salad. Slide the base onto a serving plate before cutting it into wedges.

Serves 10

Calories: 580

Fat: 12g

Saturated fat: 5g

Suitable for freezing: ✗

- Pinch saffron
- About 1.75 litres (3 pints) fish or chicken stock, hot
- 4 tablespoons sunflower oil
- 2 medium onions, peeled and sliced
- 225g ring chorizo sausage, sliced
- 750g (1½lb) paella rice
- 1 net mussels (about 1.2-1.5kg/ 3lb)
- 500g (1lb) raw shelled large prawns
- Salt and freshly ground black pepper
- 10 raw tiger prawns, shells on
- 6 cooked chicken breasts, warmed and sliced
- 1-2 tablespoons chopped fresh parsley, to garnish

- *Paella pan or frying pan*

TIPS

Paella rice is a short grain rice which is available from most supermarkets, but if you can't find it, then you could use pudding rice, although it's not exactly the same

Prawn and Chicken Paella

1 Heat a paella pan or large frying pan and very briefly cook the saffron to dry it. Remove from the pan and crumble it into the warm stock and leave it to infuse.

2 Heat the sunfower oil in the pan and add the onion and cook over a medium heat for 5-7 minutes, until it starts to soften. Add the chorizo to the pan and cook for a further 2-3 minutes, until the coloured oils start to run out of the chorizo. Add the rice to the pan and stir to coat in the onion and chorizo mixture. Pour about a third of the stock into the pan and stir it. Simmer until almost all the stock has been absorbed, stirring it occasionally. Then add half the remaining stock, stir well and continue to simmer it until that stock is amost all absorbed.

3 Meanwhile, scrub and de-beard the mussels, discarding any that do not close.

4 Add all the remaining stock to the pan and stir in the raw shelled prawns and mussels and add seasoning. Arrange the chicken on top, then place the whole prawns in shells on top. Cover the pan with a sheet of foil, or a large lid, and cook for about 5-8 minutes, until the fish is cooked.

5 Remove the lid and turn over the large shell-on prawns and cook for a little longer, if necessary, until all the prawns are cooked, and the rice is tender. If the rice dries too much, then a little boiling water can be added. Discard any mussels that don't open. Serve immediately with chopped parsley sprinkled over the top.

Pork Kebabs with Nectarines in Pancetta

Serves 4

Calories: 491

Fat: 25g

Saturated fat: 14g

Suitable for freezing: ✗

- 3 tablespoons light brown sugar
- 2 tablespoons mild olive oil
- 1½ tablespoons soy sauce
- 5 tablespoons cider or white wine vinegar
- 1 tablespoon finely grated fresh root ginger
- 2 pork tenderloins or about 750g (1½lb) boneless pork shoulder trimmed of fat and sinew, cut into 4cm (1½ in) cubes
- 2 large nectarines
- 1 tablespoon lime juice
- 8 slices of pancetta, stretched a little and halved
- 1 large onion, cut into 8 wedges, layers separate
- Tomatoes and watercress, to serve, optional

- *Metal skewers*

1. Mix the sugar, oil, soy sauce, vinegar and ginger in a large shallow dish. Add the pork cubes and use your hands to mix it in and coat the meat well. Cover and leave to marinate for 2 hours or overnight.

2. When ready to cook, thread the pork cubes onto 8 metal skewers.

3. Cook on a griddle or barbecue for 3-4 minutes each side.

4. While the pork is cooking, halve and stone the nectarines and cut each half into 4 wedges. Sprinkle them with lime juice, then wrap half a slice of pancetta round each piece.

5. Put them on separate skewers and grill them or pan fry them in a little butter and oil until just browned. Serve with sliced tomatoes and watercress, if you like.

Coffee Custards

Serves 4-6

Calories: 365

Fat: 33g

Saturated fat: 19g

Suitable for freezing: ✗

- 300ml carton double cream
- 150ml (¼ pint) whole milk
- 6 large egg yolks
- 60g (2oz) caster sugar
- 2 level tablespoons coffee granules
- Cocoa, for dusting

- *4-6 coffee cups*

1 Set the oven to 150°C or Gas Mark 2. Pour the double cream and whole milk into a pan and bring to the boil.

2 Lightly beat the egg yolks in a bowl. Pour over the boiling cream mixture, whisking as the cream is added so the eggs don't cook. Stir in the sugar until dissolved. Dissolve the coffee granules in 2 tablespoons of boiling water and add to the cream mixture.

3 Strain the cream mixture through a sieve into a jug, then pour into the coffee cups.

4 Put the cups in a roasting tin and pour in boiling water to come about halfway up the cups. Put the tin in the oven and bake for 45 minutes-1 hour, or until the mixture is just set. Remove from the oven and lift cups out of the water.

5 When the cups are cool, refrigerate well before serving, dusted with cocoa powder.

Lemon Geranium Cheesecake

Serves 10-12
Calories: 338
Fat: 30g
Saturated fat: 18g
Suitable for freezing: ✗

FOR THE BASE:
- 175g (6oz) digestive biscuits
- 90g (3oz) unsalted butter, melted

FOR THE FILLING:
- 150ml carton double cream
- 20 lemon geranium leaves
- 5 sheets leaf gelatine, softened in a bowl of water
- 150ml (¼ pint) soured cream
- 300g carton cream cheese
- 60g (2oz) caster sugar
- 2 large egg whites
- Lemon geranium leaves and flowers and violas, to decorate

- *20cm (8in) round spring-form or sandwich cake tin, buttered*

1 TO MAKE THE BASE: Crush the digestive biscuits in a bag, using a rolling pin. Mix in the melted butter. Press into the base of the tin. Leave in the fridge to set.

2 TO MAKE THE FILLING: Warm the cream with the torn geranium leaves in a pan until it just simmers. Turn off the heat and leave for 30 minutes for the flavours to infuse. Strain off and discard the leaves. Reheat the cream and add the gelatine, whisking well until dissolved. Pour into a large bowl and add the soured cream, cream cheese and sugar. Beat until smooth.

3 Whisk the egg whites to soft peaks and fold about a third into the cheese mixture, then fold in the rest. Spoon the mixture over the biscuit base. Chill until set.

4 Bring to room temperature 30 minutes before serving. Remove from the tin. Decorate the top with lemon geranium leaves and flowers, and violas.

Serves 4-6
Calories: 304
Fat: 26g
Saturated fat: 13g
Suitable for freezing: ✗

- 350g (12oz) fresh or frozen gooseberries
- 1 tablespoon elderflower cordial
- 2 tablespoons sugar, to taste
- 300ml carton double cream
- 200g cold homemade or ready-made custard
- Small gooseberries and sprigs of mint, to decorate

TIP

Not suitable for freezing but you can freeze the fruit purée for 3 months

Gooseberry Fool

1 Put the gooseberries in a pan with the cordial over a medium heat. Simmer and cook for 5-10 minutes until soft, squashing them with a spoon as they cook.

2 Purée in a food processor, then sieve to remove pips. There should be around 175-275ml (6-9fl oz) purée. Stir in the sugar. Cool completely.

3 Whip the cream to soft peaks, fold it loosely into the custard, then loosely fold in the fruit purée to give a marbled effect.

4 Spoon the mixture into glasses and chill. To serve, decorate with gooseberries and mint sprigs.

FOR THE CHOUX BUNS:
- 90g (3oz) butter, diced
- 125g (4oz) plain flour
- 3 medium eggs, beaten

FOR THE FILLING:
- Finely grated zest and juice of 2 unwaxed lemons
- 100g (3½ oz) caster sugar
- 5 tablespoons cornflour
- 3 medium egg yolks

FOR THE SAUCE:
- 125g (4oz) caster sugar
- Finely grated rind and juice 1 large lemon

- *Large heavy baking sheet, buttered and dusted with flour*

Profiteroles with Lemon Filling and Lemon Caramel Sauce

1 TO MAKE THE PROFITEROLES: Set the oven to 200°C or Gas Mark 6. Put the butter in a medium pan with 250ml (8fl oz) cold water and heat gently until the butter has melted, then bring to the boil quickly and add all the flour at once. Beat the mixture with a wooden spoon until it forms a thick paste. Cool for at least 5 minutes, then beat in the eggs a little at a time, until the mixture is smooth and shiny.

2 Use a piping bag or a dessertspoon to shape 32 balls of pastry on the baking sheet. Bake for 25 minutes until golden and crisp. Pierce each ball with a sharp knife to let the steam out, turn them over and cook for 5-10 minutes more until really crisp. Cool on a wire rack.

3 TO MAKE THE FILLING: Put the lemon zest and juice, sugar and 300ml (½ pint) cold water in a pan over a medium heat and stir until the sugar dissolves. Mix the cornflour to a smooth paste with 6 tablespoons cold water, then stir into the lemon mixture and combine well. Increase the heat, bring to the boil and cook for a couple of minutes, stirring continuously until smooth, cleared and thickened. Cool slightly, then beat in the egg yolks one at a time. Pour into a bowl, cover closely with cling film and leave until set firm and cold. When ready to fill the buns, within 3 hours of serving if possible, beat the mixture until smooth, then pipe or spoon the filling into the split choux buns. Dust with icing sugar and pile them on a plate.

4 TO MAKE THE SAUCE: Put the sugar and 4 tablespoons water in a small heavy pan. Heat gently until the sugar dissolves, then bring to the boil, without stirring, until it goes a light amber colour all over. Remove the pan from the heat and stir in the lemon juice and zest – careful, as it spatters. Stir to make a smooth sauce. Serve warm within about 10 minutes of making. It will thicken as it cools. Warm through gently for serving. The sauce may darken a little and will go stickier on reheating. Pour into a warm jug for serving.

- 6 egg whites
- 375g (13oz) caster sugar
- 1 teaspoon cornflour
- 1 teaspoon white wine vinegar
- 150g (5oz) shelled hazelnuts, skin still on, chopped

FOR THE FILLING:
- 300ml tub whipping cream
- 2 tablespoons icing sugar, plus more for dredging
- 250g (8oz) raspberries
- 125g (4oz) redcurrants

- *2 baking sheets*
- *Baking parchment*

TIP

Use plates/bowls/pan lids as a guide when drawing your circles

Raspberry and Redcurrant Hazelnut Meringue Torte

1 Set the oven to 150°C or Gas Mark 2. Draw 3 circles of about 21cm (8in), 18cm (7in) and 15cm (6in) on the baking parchment. Place on the baking sheets.

2 Whisk egg whites until stiff, whisk in half the sugar, then gradually whisk in the remainder. Mix the cornfllour and vinegar to a smooth paste and fold into the egg whites with all but 1 heaped tablespoon of the nuts. Spread the meringue in the 3 circles. Sprinkle nuts on the smallest meringue.

3 Bake for 1 hour. Turn the oven off and leave the meringues in for another hour or longer. Take out and cool.

4 TO MAKE TH FILLING: Whip the cream with the sugar until it holds its shape. Crush most of the fruit with a fork and fold into the cream to give a marble effect. Spread over the 2 larger meringues. Sandwich together, with the small meringue on top. Pop the reserved fruits round the edges. Dust with icing sugar.

Serves 6

Calories: 88

Fat: 0g

Saturated fat: 0g

Suitable for freezing: ✗

- 350ml (12fl oz) rose wine
- 2 tablespoons caster sugar
- 5 leaves gelatine
- 1 tablespoon elderflower cordial, optional
- About 600g (1¼lb) fruit: 250g (8oz) each strawberries and raspberries and 125g (4oz) blueberries

TIP

If the gelatine doesn't dissolve, put the pan back on a low heat until it does

Rose Wine and Red Berry Jellies

1 Bring about half of the wine to the simmer in a pan. Take off the heat, sprinkle in the sugar and whisk in the gelatine, 1 sheet at a time, until it dissolves.

2 Pour into a large jug, and stir in the rest of the wine and elderflower cordial, if using. Cool.

3 Pack the fruit into 6 glasses and pour in the cooled, almost-setting, wine mixture. Chill for 2 hours, or until set.

Exotic Ripple Ice Cream with Crumble Topping

Serves 8
Calories: 336
Fat: 22g
Saturated fat: 13g
Suitable for freezing: ✔

- 1 litre carton vanilla ice cream
- 200g sachet Mango & Lime Coulis
- 6 tablespoons (100g/3½oz) crumble mix

- *20cm (8in) round, loose-based sandwich cake tin, lined with cling film*

1 Spoon half of the ice cream from the tub into the lined tin. Roughly flatten it to the edges. Drizzle 5 tablespoons of the coulis over the top, then spoon in the rest of the ice cream, roughly pressing it down.

2 Cover with cling film and put in the freezer to firm for a few hours or overnight, or longer. Reseal the leftover coulis and keep in the fridge.

3 Meanwhile, set the oven to 200°C or Gas Mark 6. Spread the crumble mix out on a baking sheet and bake for 8-10 minutes until browned. Stir it halfway through cooking. Watch to see that it doesn't catch. Leave to cool.

4 To serve, take the ice-cream cake out of the tin, put on a plate and sprinkle with crumble mix. Cut into wedges and serve drizzled with the rest of the coulis.

❋ *Can be kept frozen at the end of step 1, but if being kept for more than a day or two, then freeze the coulis, too. Cook the crumble topping on day of serving, allowing frozen coulis to defrost for a couple of hours*

Serves 5-6

Calories: 666

Fat: 57g

Saturated fat: 27g

Suitable for freezing: ✗

- 375g packet ready-rolled puff pastry
- 3-4 level tablespoons strawberry jam
- 250-350g (8-12oz) strawberries
- 300ml carton double cream
- 250g carton mascarpone cheese
- ½ vanilla pod, or a few drops vanilla extract.
- Icing sugar, for dusting

- *Baking sheets*
- *Icing bag with large star piping tube*

Strawberry Millefeuilles

1 Set the oven to 220°C or Gas Mark 7. Unroll the pastry and trim off the edges. Cut into 3 strips widthways and place on a baking sheet. Prick the surface of the pastry with a fork. A tip of ensuring the pastry rises evenly is to place another baking sheet on top, supported on metal weights, or cubes of potato.

2 Bake the pastry, in the top of the oven, for about 15 minutes, until it is a light golden colour. Remove from the oven and transfer the pastry to wire racks and leave to cool.

3 Lightly whip the double cream and fold in the double cream. Add the seeds scraped from the vanilla pod or a few drops vanilla extract and fold in. Fill a piping bag fitted with the star piping tube with the cream mixture.

4 Trim the edges of the pastry rectangles to neaten them. Spread the strawberry jam over two layers of the pastry. Pipe the cream mixture over the jam, piping the edges first so that they are neat, then filling in the centre with the remaining mixture.

5 Reserve 5-6 strawberries for the top decoration and slice the remaining strawberries. Stack the slice, with the plain sheet of pastry on the top.

6 Dredge the icing sugar heavily over the top. If you like, a pattern may be scorched on the top by heating a skewer with a gas flame and then pressing it over the icing sugar. Wipe the skewer clean between each heating – and take care not to burn your fingers.

7 Halve the reserved strawberries and arrange them in a line down the top.

Battenberg Cake

Serves 8-10

Calories: 462

Fat: 21g

Saturated fat: 9g

Suitable for freezing: ✗

- 175g (6oz) butter, softened
- 175g (6oz) caster sugar
- 3 medium eggs
- 175g (6oz) self-raising flour
- 2 tablespoons milk
- A few drops red liquid food colouring
- 10-12 tablespoons apricot glaze, or sieved apricot jam
- 350g (12oz) white marzipan

- *18 x 28cm (7 x 11in) oblong tin, lined with baking parchment*

1 Set the oven to 180°C or Gas Mark 4. Cut a length of baking parchment the length of the tin and fold in half, so that it's just higher than the tin.

2 Cream the butter and caster sugar together until the mixture is light and fluffy, then beat in the eggs, adding a dessertspoon of flour with each egg to help prevent the mixture curdling. Fold in the remaining flour and the milk.

3 Spoon half of the mixture into one half of the tin, lengthways, then place the strip of baking parchment in the tin, to keep the two colours of sponge separate during cooking. Colour the remaining cake mixture pink with the red or pink food colouring and spoon into the other half of the tin. Level the surface of the cake.

4 Bake in the centre of the oven for 25-30 minutes, or until well risen and firm to the touch in the centre. Remove the cake from the oven and leave to cool in the tin for 5-10 minutes, then turn out onto a wire rack and leave to cool completely.

5 Cut the cake in half lengthways to separate the colours of the cake, trimming away the long edges, and neatening the lines where the cakes were touching, if necessary. Cut these strips in half again, to give 4 strips (2 of each colour). Use a palette knife to spread a little apricot jam over the cake and stick them together in the chequerboard pattern.

6 Roll the marzipan out on a surface lightly dusted with icing sugar, to the length of the cake, and just over 4 times the width. Place the cake onto the marzipan and roll the cake up in the marzipan, trimming away any excess at the join..

7 Use a small knife to mark a criss-cross pattern on the top of the cake, then press a fork down the length of each side on the top to pattern it. Cut off both ends to neaten the cake before serving.

Ginger Shortcake

Serves 8

Calories: 125

Fat: 13g

Saturated fat: 5g

Suitable for freezing: ✗

- 125g (4oz) butter
- 60g (2oz) caster sugar
- 150g (5oz) plain flour
- 1 level teaspoon baking powder
- 1 level teaspoon ground ginger

FOR THE ICING:

- 4 rounded tablespoons icing sugar, sifted
- 60g (2oz) butter
- 1 level teaspoon ground ginger
- 3 level teaspoons golden syrup

- *20cm (8in) round sandwich tin (preferably loose-bottomed), buttered and base lined*

1 Set the oven to 160°C or Gas Mark 3. Beat the butter to a soft cream, then beat in the caster sugar – they must be very well beaten together.

2 Sift the flour, baking powder and the ground ginger, then mix this into the creamed mixture. Spread the mixture into the buttered tin.

3 Bake in the centre of the oven for about 40 minutes. While the shortcake is still hot in the tin, put the ingredients for the icing into a saucepan and melt them together.

4 Pour this mixture over the top of the shortcake and spread it evenly.

5 Leave the shortcake in the tin and cut it into pieces while it's still warm. When cold, ease the slices out with a knife, mark a curved pattern on each slice with the prongs of a fork.

Makes 32-36

Calories: 225

Fat: 15g

Saturated fat: 9g

Suitable for freezing: ✗

- 150g (5oz) butter, softened
- 150g (5oz) golden caster sugar
- 3 medium eggs
- 150g (5oz) self-raising flour
- Finely grated zest and juice of 1 lemon

FOR THE BUTTERCREAM:
- 250g (8oz) butter, softened
- 500g (1lb) icing sugar, sieved
- A few drops of rose water, optional
- 250g carton mascarpone cheese
- Pink terracotta and grape violet paste food colouring
- Crystallised rose petals and violets, to decorate

- *3 x 12-hole mini muffin trays, lined with paper cases*
- *Piping bag and star nozzle*

TIP

If you would prefer regular-sized cupcakes, then this mixture will make 12

Roses are Red, Violets are Blue Mini Cupcakes

1 Set the oven to 190°C or Gas Mark 5. Mix the butter and golden caster sugar in a bowl with an electric mixer, until light and fluffy. Gradually beat in the eggs, fold in the flour and lemon zest and juice. Gently mix until smooth. Divide the mixture between the paper cases.

2 Bake in the centre of the oven for 10-15 minutes, until risen and firm to the touch in the centre. Take out of the oven and put cupcakes a wire rack to cool completely.

3 TO MAKE THE BUTTERCREAM: Beat the butter to soften it, preferably using an electric whisk, then slowly add the icing sugar, rose water, if using, and mascarpone cheese and beat until smooth.

4 Divide the mixture between 2 bowls. Colour a batch pink and the other violet by dipping a cocktail stick into the paste food colourings and mixing it in until evenly coloured. Pipe large swirls of the buttercream on top of the cooled cupcakes, using the piping bag and star nozzle. Top with crystallised roses and violets.

Cherry and Almond Cake

Cuts into 12 slices

Calories: 453

Fat: 28g

Saturated fat: 12g

Suitable for freezing: ✔

- 250g (8oz) butter, softened
- 250g (8oz) caster sugar
- 4 medium eggs
- 250g (8oz) plain flour
- A few drops of almond extract
- 1 level teaspoon baking powder
- 200g carton glace cherries, halved
- 125g (4oz) ground almonds
- 4 tablespoons milk
- 50g (1¾oz) flaked almonds
- Icing sugar, for dusting

- 20cm (8in) round cake tin, lined with baking parchment

1 Set the oven to 160° or Gas Mark 3. Place an oven shelf just below the centre of the oven so that the cake will be central in the oven.

2 Beat together the butter and caster sugar until the mixture is light and fluffy. Beat in the eggs, one at a time along with a spoonful of flour with each egg. Pour in the almond extract.

3 Sift the remaining flour and baking powder over the mixture and fold it in, then fold in the cherries, ground almonds and milk. Spoon the mixture into the lined cake tin and level the surface. Sprinkle over the flaked almonds.

4 Bake the cake in the centre of the oven for 1¼-1½ hours, or until the cake has risen and is just firm to the touch in the centre.

5 Remove the cake from the oven and leave it to cool in the tin for at least 30 minutes, then transfer it to a wire rack to cool completely.

6 Dust the top of the cake with icing sugar just before serving it, then cut into 12 slices.

❄ *Wrap the cold cake in a freezer bag and freeze the cake for up to 1 month. Allow the cake to defrost for a few hours before dusting over the icing sugar to serve*

Makes 16

Calories: 170

Fat: 3g

Saturated fat: 1.2g

Suitable for freezing: ✗

- 16 biscuits – shortbread, for example – homemade or bought

FOR THE ICING:
- 100g (3½oz) redcurrants
- 300g (10oz) icing sugar

TIP

This icing is also good on almond biscuits

Berried Biscuits

1 TO MAKE THE ICING: Put the redcurrants and icing sugar into the bowl of a food processor and add 1 teaspoon water, then blend well.

2 Press the icing through a sieve to remove any redcurrant seeds.

3 Spoon the icing onto the biscuits and leave to set before serving.

STARTERS

MAIN MEALS

DESSERTS

TEATIME TREATS

AUTUMN

Caramelised Red Onion Quiche

Makes 4

Calories: 693

Fat: 57g

Saturated fat: 33g

Suitable for freezing: ✗

FOR THE PASTRY:
- 150g (5oz) wholemeal flour
- Pinch of salt
- 100g (3½oz) unsalted butter

FOR THE FILLING:
- 30g (1oz) butter
- 1 tablespoon light olive oil
- 500g (1lb) red onions, peeled and sliced
- 1 level teaspoon caster sugar
- 1 level tablespoon freshly chopped thyme
- Salt and freshly ground black pepper
- 2 medium eggs
- 170ml carton double cream
- 1 tablespoon Dijon mustard

- *4 x 12cm (4½in) flan tins*

1 Tip the flour and salt into the bowl of a food processor and add butter. Whizz until breadcrumbs form. Add 1-2 tablespoons water and whizz until mixture just starts to bind together into a dough.

2 Divide the mixture into 4 and roll each one out. Use to line the tins. Chill cases for 30 minutes.

3 TO PREPARE THE FILLING: Melt the butter in a pan and add the oil. Stir in onion and sprinkle over sugar. Cook for about 20-30 minutes, stirring occasionally, until onion softens and caramelises. Remove pan from hob, so onions cool slightly.

4 Set the oven to 190°C or Gas Mark 5. Heat a baking sheet.

5 Divide the onion mixture between the pastry cases. Sprinkle over the thyme and season with salt and pepper to taste. Beat the eggs with the cream and mustard and pour into the pastry cases.

6 Place the tarts on the baking sheet and cook in the oven for 35-40 minutes, or until set. When cooked, transfer to a wire rack. Leave to cool for a few minutes, then remove from the tins and cool. Serve warm or at room temperature.

TIP

For an extra tang, spread a little red onion relish on pastry case before adding the filling

Zesty Crab with Melba Toast

Serves 4

Calories: 178

Fat: 14g

Saturated fat: 7g

Suitable for freezing: ✗

- 100g (3½oz) white crabmeat
- 125-150g (4-5oz) cooked king prawns, chopped
- 4 spring onions, finely sliced
- 2 level tablespoons freshly chopped dill
- 1 tablespoon virgin olive oil
- Finely zested rind of ½ lemon
- Salt and freshly ground black pepper
- ½ x 200ml carton crème fraîche
- Salmon caviar and sprigs of dill, to garnish
- Melba toast, to serve

- *4 metal rings, 7cm (2¾in) in diameter, oiled*

1 Line a small baking tray with cling film and place the 4 metal rings on the tray.

2 Place the crabmeat, prawns, spring onion, dill, olive oil, lemon rind and seasoning in a bowl and mix well. Divide the mixture between the 4 rings, pressing it down firmly.

3 Stir the crème fraîche to soften it and spread it over the top of the fish mixture. Chill for at least 2 hours, or overnight.

4 To serve, slide a wide palette knife under each ring in turn and transfer them to a plate. Lift off the ring.

5 Garnish with a little salmon caviar and a sprig of dill, and serve with Melba toast.

Serves 6
Calories: 345
Fat: 12g
Saturated fat: 3g
Suitable for freezing: ✗

- 300g (10oz) lamb neck fillet
- 2 tablespoons medium balti curry paste
- 1 tablespoon olive oil
- 1 medium onion, peeled and roughly chopped
- 1 large carrot, peeled
- 1 parsnip, peeled
- 1 medium potato, peeled
- 1 red pepper, deseeded
- 500g carton passata
- 900ml (1½ pints) hot lamb, chicken or vegetable stock
- Salt and freshly ground black pepper
- 180g pack frozen cooked basmati rice
- Fresh coriander, to garnish

FOR THE POTATO WEDGES:
- 3 large baking potatoes
- 2 tablespoons vegetable oil
- 2 teaspoons cumin seeds

Mulligatawny with Spicy Potato Wedges

1 Set the oven to 200°C or Gas Mark 6. Rub the lamb all over with 2 teaspoons of the curry paste. Put in a roasting tin, cover with foil, and roast for 45 minutes. Set aside to rest for 10 minutes or longer, then shred the meat.

2 Meanwhile, heat the oil in a large pan over a low heat, add the onion and cook for 5 minutes until softened. Chop the carrot and parsnip into thick slices and the potato and pepper into 1cm (½in) chunks. Add to the pan and cook for a few minutes.

3 Increase the heat and stir in the rest of the curry paste, cook for 2 minutes, stirring, then pour in the passata and the stock. Season to taste, bring to the boil, then reduce the heat, cover and simmer for 20 minutes, or until the veg are just tender. Add the rice and shredded lamb and heat through. Serve sprinkled with torn coriander leaves.

4 TO MAKE THE POTATO WEDGES: Scrub the potatoes and cut into wedges (5-6 per person). Brush them all over with oil, put on a Teflon-lined baking sheet, sprinkle them with cumin seeds. Roast in the oven for 45 minutes while the lamb is cooking, turning them halfway through cooking.

Soya Bean, Spinach and Pea Soup

Serves 4

Calories: 150

Fat: 6g

Saturated fat: 0.5g

Suitable for freezing: ✔

- 200g (7oz) frozen soya beans
- 200g (7oz) frozen peas
- 600ml (1 pint) hot vegetable stock
- 5 spring onions, trimmed and chopped
- 2 basil leaves
- 1 handful (about 60g/2oz) of fresh baby spinach leaves
- 300ml (½ pint) soya milk or regular milk
- Salt and freshly ground black pepper
- Several small basil leaves, to garnish, optional

1 Put the frozen beans and peas into a pan. Pour in the vegetable stock and add the spring onions, basil and spinach.

2 Bring to the boil, then simmer for 10 minutes until the beans and peas are tender.

3 Pour half of the soup into a blender and whizz until smooth. Return to the pan with the milk and warm through. Season with salt and freshly ground black pepper. Serve garnished with basil leaves, if you like.

※ *May be frozen for up to 1 month. Allow to defrost before reheating thoroughly*

TIP

You'll find the frozen soya beans next to the frozen peas in supermarkets. Substitute with frozen broad beans if you prefer, or if unable to find soya beans

Garlic Mushrooms on Toasted Brioche

Serves 2-3

Calories per serving: 360

Fat per serving: 24g

Suitable for freezing: ✗

- 300g (10oz) mixed mushrooms –
  portabellini, crimini, shiitake
- 30g (1oz) butter
- 2 teaspoons olive oil
- 2 shallots, peeled and
  finely chopped
- 1 large clove garlic, peeled
  and crushed
- Freshly ground black pepper
- 2 tablespoons Marsala or
  medium sherry
- 1 tablespoon chopped
  fresh tarragon
- 4-6 slices brioche or other rich
  bread dough loaf, toasted
- 6 tablespoons crème fraîche

1 Clean the mushrooms with a small brush or wipe them over with kitchen paper.

2 Heat half the butter and oil in a frying-pan, add the shallots and garlic and cook over a low heat for 5 minutes until softened but not browned.

3 Add the rest of the butter, the olive oil and the mushrooms. Season to taste with some freshly ground black pepper, cover and cook for 5-8 minutes, stirring occasionally, until the mushrooms are just cooked.

4 Take off the lid and stir in the Marsala or sherry and tarragon and cook for 2-3 minutes, until the liquid is syrupy. Spoon the mushrooms on to the toasted brioche using a slotted spoon. Stir the crème fraîche into the pan juices and heat through, then spoon over the mushrooms.

Seafood Pasties

Makes 18

Calories each: 110

Fat: 6g

Saturated fat: 3g

Suitable for freezing: ✗

- 270g pack filo pastry (6 sheets)
- 90g (3oz) butter
- 1 tablespoon sesame seeds, optional

FOR THE FILLING:
- 150g (5oz) butternut squash, finely diced
- 4 spring onions, trimmed and sliced
- 180g carton of mussels in brine, drained, or a pack of fresh mussels
- 10g jar of cockles, drained
- 1 tablespoon white wine vinegar or 1 tablespoon Thai curry paste
- 1 tablespoon butter, melted
- Salt and freshly ground black pepper
- 1 tablespoon chopped fresh parsley or coriander

- *Large baking sheet, lined with baking parchment*

1 Mix together all the filling ingredients. Set the oven to 200°C or Gas Mark 6.

2 Lay out 1 sheet of filo pastry at a time. Brush it with butter, then cut it into 3 long strips. Put a good tablespoonful of filling at the base of each strip, then fold it up and over in the pastry in a triangle shape, and keep on folding until you get to the top. Put the pasties on the baking sheet and brush with butter. Sprinkle with sesame seeds, if using. Bake for 30 minutes until the pastry is golden and crisp. Serve hot or cold.

TIP

To make these piquant, add vinegar and parsley to the filling, or, for a Thai flavour, add curry paste and coriander. You can add fresh or canned baby clams instead of the cockles

Serves 2

Calories: 522	
Fat: 47g	
Saturated fat: 11g	
Suitable for freezing: ✗	

- 4 tablespoons light olive oil
- 4 rashers smoked streaky bacon, chopped
- 2 slices black pudding (½ x 115g packet), diced
- 1 tablespoon wholegrain mustard
- 2 tablespoons red wine vinegar
- Salt and freshly ground black pepper
- 80-120g bag salad leaves
- 2 poached eggs

Egg, Black Pudding and Bacon Salad

1 Heat 2 tablespoons olive oil in a frying pan. Add the chopped bacon to the pan and cook for 2-3 minutes. Add the black pudding to the pan and cook until the bacon is crispy and the black pudding is heated through, then remove the pan from the heat.

2 Mix the remaining olive oil with the wholegrain mustard, red wine vinegar, salt and freshly ground black pepper. Stir to mix them all together and add to the pan.

3 Divide the salad leaves between 2 plates and spoon the bacon and black pudding over the top. Pour the juices in the pan over it, as a salad dressing.

4 Top each salad with a poached egg, then grind over some black pepper. Serve immediately.

Baked Cheese with Maple Syrup Glaze

Serves 2

Calories: 690

Fat: 54g

Saturated fat: 22g

Suitable for freezing: ✗

- 200g round Golden Cenarth cheese in a box
- 1 tablespoon olive oil
- A few sprigs thyme
- 50g (1¾oz) roasted and salted pecan nuts, roughly chopped
- 2 tablespoons light muscovado sugar
- 2 tablespoons amber maple syrup
- Crusty bread, to serve

1 Set the oven to 200°C or Gas Mark 6. Remove the plastic from the cheese and replace it in its box.

2 Put the cheese a baking tray. Cut some slashes in the top, drizzle the olive oil and scatter the thyme over it. Bake the cheese for 10-15 minutes, or until it starts to ooze.

3 Spread the nuts out on another baking tray and heat them through in the oven for 4-5 minutes.

4 Put the sugar and maple syrup in a small pan and place over a low heat, stirring until the sugar melts. Bring to the boil, then simmer for a few minutes until it's thickened slightly.

5 Stir half of the nuts into the syrup and pour over the baked cheese, then scatter over the remaining nuts. Serve with crusty bread to scoop into the runny cheese.

TIP

An alternative to the Golden Cenarth cheese is to use a whole Somerset Camembert or Cornish Brie. Mini cheeses can also be used for individual servings

Poachers' Pies

Serves 4

Calories: 936	
Fat: 52	
Saturated fat: 24	
Suitable for freezing: ✗	

- 250g (8oz) self-raising flour
- 125g (4oz) vegetable suet
- 2 tablespoons fresh chopped parsley
- Beaten egg, to glaze
- 2 teaspoons sesame seeds, optional

FOR THE FILLING:
- 1 whole rabbit, jointed (a rabbit weighs about 1.5kg/3lb), or 8 rabbit joints
- 15g (½oz) butter
- 4 rashers lean bacon, each cut into quarters
- 4-6 shallots, peeled and halved
- 1 large carrot, peeled and sliced into batons
- 1 fennel bulb, cut into wedges
- 2 cloves garlic, peeled and sliced
- 150ml (¼ pint) dry sherry/Madeira or white wine
- 600ml (1 pint) chicken stock
- Bay leaf and thyme sprigs
- Salt and freshly ground black pepper
- 12 olives (green, black or mixed, stoned, if you prefer)

- *4 x 300ml (½ pint) capacity ovenproof dishes*

1 TO MAKE THE FILLING: Brown the rabbit portions in half the butter in a pan for about 5 minutes. Take out of the pan. Add the rest of the butter, the bacon, shallots, carrot, fennel and garlic, and any liver/heart, and brown for about 5 minutes.

2 Pour in the sherry or white wine and stock, and bring to the boil. Add the bay and thyme sprigs to the pan, then the rabbit portions. Season, cover and cook over a low heat for 1-1½ hours until tender.

3 Using a draining spoon, remove the rabbit and vegetables from the pan and leave to cool for a few minutes. Put the cooking juices in the pan back on the heat, boil and reduce to about 600ml (1 pint). Take the meat off the bones (there should be about 600g (1¼lb).

4 Set the oven to 200°C or Gas Mark 6. Put the rabbit meat back in the juices and heat with the vegetables for a few minutes, while you make the pastry topping.

5 TO MAKE THE SUET PASTRY TOPPING: Mix the flour, vegetable suet, seasoning and parsley with about 150ml (¼ pint) water to bind, then add 2-3 tablespoons water, to make a soft dough. Divide the dough into 4 and pat each one out with your hand to fit the top of the dishes.

6 Spoon the hot meat, vegetables, and olives into the 4 dishes with enough juice to come almost to the top.

7 Damp the dish edges with water and fit the pastry lid on. Brush with egg and sprinkle with sesame seeds, if using.

8 Bake the pies, on a baking tray, for 30 minutes. Serve with any leftover cooking juices reheated.

TIP
Try using celery or leeks instead of fennel, if you prefer

Spanish Chicken with Beans

Serves 2-4

Calories: 450

Fat: 22g

Saturated fat: 6g

Suitable for freezing: ✔

- 1 tablespoon olive oil
- 4 chicken thighs, with skin (about 600g (1¼lb)
- 125g (4oz) chorizo, skinned and sliced
- 1 onion, peeled and sliced
- 1 red pepper, deseeded and chopped
- 1 clove garlic, peeled and crushed
- 1 tablespoon red pesto (or sun-dried tomato paste)
- 410g can cannelloni beans, drained and rinsed
- 300ml (1½ pint) hot chicken stock
- Few sprigs thyme
- 1 level teaspoon smoked paprika

1 Heat the oil in a deep frying pan. Add the chicken thighs, skin-side down, the chorizo and onion.

2 Cook the chicken for 5 minutes without turning it over to allow the skin to brown, but stir the onion and chorizo.

3 Turn the chicken over and the red pepper, garlic, red pesto or sun-dried tomato paste, cannelloni beans, stock and thyme. Sprinkle the smoked paprika on top of the chicken.

4 Bring to the boil, cover and simmer for 25 minutes, until the chicken is tender.

❊ *When cold, pack into a suitable container and freeze for up to 1 month. Allow to defrost before reheating thoroughly.*

TIP

Add a few green olives for even more Mediterranean flavour

Serves 8

Calories: 470

Fat: 24g

Saturated fat: 13g

Suitable for freezing: ✔

- 1 butternut squash, peeled and cut into cubes (about 750g/1½lb prepared weight)
- 2 onions, peeled and cut into thin wedges
- 2-3 carrots, peeled and chopped
- 16 large sage leaves
- 2 tablespoons olive oil
- 750ml (1¼ pint) milk
- 60g (2oz) plain flour
- 60g (2oz) butter
- Freshly grated nutmeg
- 200g (7oz) mature Cheddar cheese, grated
- Salt and freshly ground black pepper
- 200g (7oz) frozen green beans, chopped into short lengths 250g pack dried lasagne or 300g pack fresh lasagne strips
- 60g (2oz) Parmesan, grated

- *1.75 litre (3 pint) ovenproof dish*

Butternut Squash Lasagne

1 Set the oven to 230°C or Gas Mark 8. Spread the squash, onion, chopped carrots and 8 sage leaves out in a large roasting tin. Drizzle with olive oil and roast in the oven for 30-40 minutes.

2 TO MAKE THE CHEESE SAUCE: Pour the milk into a large jug, whisk in the flour, then add the butter. Microwave on High for 4 minutes, stir, cook for another 4 minutes, stir, then cook for 3-4 minutes longer, until thick and smooth. Chop the rest of the sage and add to the sauce, along with the nutmeg and two-thirds of the Cheddar cheese. Season wtih salt and freshly ground black pepper. Thaw the green beans in the microwave.

3 Spoon some sauce in the dish. Put in a few sheets of lasagne, then a third, or half, of the squash mixture (depending on shape of your dish), beans and a little more sauce. Continue with lasagne sheets, squash mixture and beans. End with a good layer of sauce. Sprinkle with the rest of the cheese. TO SERVE NOW: Set the oven to 200°C or Gas Mark 6. Bake the lasagne for 45-50 minutes until golden and piping hot.

❋ *To freeze uncooked: Cool, wrap well and freeze for up to 2 months. Thaw in the fridge overnight. Bake as above.*

Lamb and Sultana Tikka Biriyani

Serves 4

Calories: 551

Fat: 23g

Saturated fat: 6g

Suitable for freezing: ✗

- 2 tablespoons sunflower oil
- 2 onions, peeled and sliced
- 30g (1oz) sultanas
- 400g (14oz) diced leg of lamb
- 3 cloves garlic, crushed
- 1cm (½in) piece fresh ginger, peeled and grated
- 2 tablespoons ground almonds
- 4 tablespoons tikka curry paste
- 250ml (8fl oz) plain yogurt
- 1 x 0.4g sachet saffron threads
- 2 tablespoons milk, warmed
- 200g (7oz) basmati rice
- 1 teaspoon salt

1 Set the oven to 190°C or Gas Mark 5. Heat 1 tablespoon oil in a flameproof casserole and fry the onion until golden. Add the sultanas and cook for a few minutes. Take out half the mixture and set aside.

2 Add the lamb and cook for 10 minutes, stirring occasionally, until browned all over. Meanwhile, put the crushed garlic, grated ginger, ground almonds and 2 tablespoons water into a small blender and whizz until smooth.

3 Add the tikka curry paste to the lamb, cook for 1 minute, then add the garlic mixture, along with 200ml (7fl oz) water and the yogurt. Stir well, cover and cook in the oven for 1 hour, until the meat is tender.

4 Put the saffron into a cup, add the warm milk and leave to infuse.

5 After 40 minutes, put the rice into a pan with the salt and 400ml (14fl oz) water. Cover and cook for 15 minutes, until the liquid is absorbed and the rice is tender.

6 To serve, pile the rice on top of the lamb tikka, push a wooden spoon handle into the centre of the rice to make a hole. Pour in saffron milk, then stir the rice and lamb tikka together. Spoon the reserved onions and sultanas on top.

TIP

Saffron is the most expensive spice in the world – turmeric can be used as a substitute to give a yellow colour

Serves 4
Calories: 420
Fat: 11g
Saturated fat: 3g
Suitable for freezing: ✗

- 1 tablespoon olive oil
- 100g (3½oz) smoked bacon lardoons
- 1 onion, peeled and finely chopped
- 1 teaspoon smoked paprika
- 2 cloves garlic, peeled and crushed
- 200g (7oz) Camargue red rice
- 400g can chopped tomatoes
- 600ml (1 pint) hot fish or chicken stock
- 1 red pepper, deseeded and chopped
- 200g (7oz) squid, cut into rings
- 200g (7oz) scallops
- 8 raw king prawns
- Parsley and lemon wedges, to serve

TIP

If you like, replace the red rice with risotto rice or a mixture of basmati and wild rice

Provence in a Pan

1 Heat a deep frying pan with the olive oil and add the lardoons and onion. Fry over a medium heat for about 5 minutes, until the bacon is crispy.

2 Stir in the smoked paprika and garlic cloves, then add the rice. Stir-fry for 1 minute, then pour in the chopped tomatoes and stock. Bring to the boil, cover and simmer for 20 minutes.

3 Add the red pepper to the pan and simmer for 10 minutes, stirring occasionally, then add the squid, scallops and prawns and stir into the rice, so they're all under the liquid. Simmer for about 5 minutes, until the prawns turn pink. The consistency should still be soupy and the rice al dente. Garnish with chopped parsley and serve with lemon wedges.

Serves 2

Calories per serving: 324

Fat per serving: 17g

Saturated fat: 6g

Suitable for freezing: ✗

- 1 tablespoon olive oil
- 1 red pepper, deseeded and finely diced
- 3 sticks celery, chopped
- 1 clove garlic, peeled and chopped
- 4 spring onions, trimmed and chopped
- 1 teaspoon chopped fresh thyme or 1 tablespoon chopped fresh parsley
- Salt and freshly ground black pepper
- 8 sheets filo pastry
- 1 medium egg white, lightly beaten
- 60g (2oz) Blue Shropshire cheese, crumbled
- 2 teaspoons sesame seeds

Mixed Vegetable Parcels

1 Set the oven to 200°C or Gas Mark 6. Heat a non-stick frying pan, add the olive oil, pepper, celery and garlic and cook for 3-4 minutes, until lightly coloured. Stir in the spring onions and herbs. Season with salt and freshly ground black pepper. Set aside to cool.

2 Brush 1 sheet of pastry with a little egg white. Lay a second sheet at right angles over the first, brush with egg white. Repeat with another 2 sheets at right angles. Spoon half the vegetables into the centre of the pastry and top with half the cheese.

3 Gather up the ends of the pastry to form a parcel, press tightly together in the middle with your finger tips to seal. Carefully pull out the top a little so the pastry is not too thick. Put the parcel on a baking sheet. Brush with egg white and sprinkle with seeds. Make another parcel. Bake about 20 minutes until golden. Serve with salad and new potatoes.

Serves 2-4

Calories: 105

Fat: 5g

Saturated fat: 1g

Suitable for freezing: ✗

- 2 shallots, peeled and finely chopped
- 2 cloves garlic, peeled and crushed
- 1 chilli, seeds removed, finely chopped
- ½ teaspoon each ground turmeric, ground coriander and ground cumin
- 1 tablespoon soy sauce
- 1 tablespoon sunflower oil
- 200g (7oz) pork fillet, cut in thin strips

TO SERVE:
- 250g (8oz) Jasmine rice
- Pinch of salt
- Radishes, 4 trimmed and chopped, and 2 carved
- ½ cucumber; ¼ chopped and ¼ cut into ribbons
- 1 tablespoon fresh coriander
- 4 x 150ml (5fl oz) dariole moulds, oiled
- 12 bamboo skewers, soaked in water

Indonesian Pork Skewers

1 Put the shallots in a shallow dish. Add the garlic, chilli, ground turmeric, coriander and cumin, soy sauce and the sunflower oil. Add the pork fillet and stir to coat in the marinade. Leave for 30 minutes for the flavours to penetrate.

2 Put the Jasmine rice into a pan with the salt and 600ml (1 pint) boiling water. Bring to the boil and cook for 15 minutes, until the rice is tender and the liquid absorbed. Spoon into the dariole moulds and put them in a warm place for a few minutes.

3 Meanwhile, set the grill to high. Thread the strips of pork on to the bamboo skewers. Grill for about 15 minutes, turning them as needed, until they are browned all over.

4 Carefully turn the cooked rice out of the dariole moulds on to a tray. Serve the pork on the skewers, along with a bowl of chopped radishes and cucumber, garnished with coriander leaves. Decorate the serving plates with ribbons of cucumber and carved radishes.

Farmhouse Fry-up

Serves 3

Calories: 221

Fat: 12g

Saturated fat: 2.5g

Suitable for freezing: ✗

- 4 teaspoons rapeseed oil
- 300g (10oz) cooked potatoes, sliced
- 250g (8oz) mushrooms, sliced
- 100g (3½oz) chard, torn
- 3 medium eggs
- Oil flavoured with chilli flakes, optional
- Parmesan or Cheddar shavings, to serve
- Baguette, to serve

1 Warm 2 teaspoons rapeseed oil in a pan, add the sliced potatoes and sauté over a medium heat for 4-5 minutes, until browned. Remove from the pan and set aside. Add the remaining 2 teaspoons oil to the pan, along with the sliced mushrooms. Put the lid on the pan and place over a medium heat for 5 minutes.

2 Remove lid, turn up the heat and fry until the liquid is absorbed and the mushrooms are browned. Put the potatoes back in. Add the chard leaves, wilt for a minute, then break in the eggs. Replace the lid and cook until the eggs have just set. Drizzle with a little oil flavoured with dried chilli flakes, if you like.

3 Serve with shavings of Parmesan or Cheddar and hunks of baguette.

TIP

If you prefer, you can use spring cabbage or ready-chopped kale instead of chard

Upside-down Chocolate Pear Pudding

Serves 12
Calories: 248
Fat: 12g
Saturated fat: 8g
Suitable for freezing: ✗

- 60g (2oz) caster sugar
- 1 tablespoon lemon juice
- A dash of vanilla extract
- 4 ripe pears, peeled, halved and cored
- 150g (5oz) plain chocolate
- 4 tablespoons milk
- 90g (3oz) butter, softened
- 90g (3oz) light muscovado sugar
- 2 medium eggs
- 90g (3oz) self-raising flour
- 30g (1oz) ground almonds
- Icing sugar, for dredging, optional

- *20cm (8in) loose-based sandwich tin, greased and base-lined*

1 Put the sugar, lemon juice, vanilla extract and 600ml (1 pint) cold water in a large, shallow pan. Bring to the boil gradually, stirring occasionally, until the sugar has dissolved. Add the pears and simmer gently for 10-15 minutes until just tender. Spoon the pears out onto a plate and leave them to cool. Keep the syrup in the pan.

2 Set the oven to 190°C or Gas Mark 5. Use a swivel-headed potato peeler to grate some chocolate for decorating the cake – about 30g (1oz). Set this aside on a plate and cover.

3 Put the rest of the chocolate in a small bowl with the milk and melt over a pan of gently simmering water (or in the microwave) until smooth.

4 Arrange the drained pear halves, cut side down, in the bottom of the tin.

5 Beat the butter and brown sugar until light and fluffy. Gradually beat in the eggs one at a time, adding a couple of tablespoons of flour as well.

6 Stir in the melted chocolate, then the rest of the flour. Add the ground almonds. Fold in gently. Spoon the mixture over the pears, smoothing the top. Bake for about 40 minutes, until a skewer inserted comes out clean. Leave to cool in the tin for 15 minutes.

7 Meanwhile, reduce the poaching liquid to about 100ml (3½fl oz) and syrupy. Before taking the pudding out of the tin, make holes in it with a skewer and spoon over the syrup, letting it soak in completely.

8 Turn out the pudding. Sprinkle with the grated chocolate. Dust with a little sifted icing sugar, if you like. Serve warm or cold with cream.

Autumn Pudding

Serves 6

Calories: 351

Fat: 1.3g

Saturated fat: 0.7g

Suitable for freezing: ✗

- 175g (6oz) caster sugar
- 1kg (2¼lb) mixed prepared fruits – blackberries and apples
- 10-12 slices white bread, medium sliced, crusts removed
- Clotted cream, to serve

- 9.5cm (3¾in) plain, round cutter
- 1.5 litre (2½ pint) pudding basin

1. Pour 6 tablespoons water into a pan and add the sugar. Place the pan over a medium heat and stir until the sugar dissolves. Add the fruits and simmer on a low heat for 7-10 minutes, until the fruit is soft.

2. Strain the fruit through a sieve to separate the juice. Cut a round out of 1 slice of bread to fit the base of the pudding basin. Dip one side of the bread in the juice and put in the basin, dipped-side down. Reserve 4 slices to cover the top. Cut the rest of the slices of bread into 3 strips. Dip each strip in the juice and place against the sides of the basin at a slight angle and overlapping them slightly.

3. Spoon the fruit mixture into the basin, pressing it down well. Pour most of the remaining juice on top, or as much as the bowl will take. Cover the top with the reserved bread and cut away the excess around the edge of the bowl. Brush the rest of the juice over the top of the bread.

4. Put the pudding basin in a shallow bowl to catch any juices that may leak out. Cover the pudding with a layer of cling film, then put a plate on top with about 1kg (2¼lb) weights (or cans of fruit or beans) on top. Put in the fridge overnight to chill the pudding well.

5. To serve, remove the plate with the weights and the cling film. Place a serving plate, with a rim to catch any juices, over the top of the pudding, invert the plate and shake hard to release it. Serve with clotted cream.

Serves 4

Calories: 600
Fat: 16g
Saturated fat: 9g
Suitable for freezing: ✗

FOR THE SAUCE:
- 30g (1oz) butter
- 90g (3oz) light soft brown sugar
- 2 tablespoons golden syrup
- 142ml carton double cream
- 2 tablespoons Calvados

FOR THE FRITTERS:
- 60g (2oz) plain flour
- 30g (1oz) caster sugar
- ½ level teaspoon ground cinnamon
- 1 medium egg, separated
- 2-3 apples, peeled, cored and thickly sliced

- *Deep-frying pan with sunflower oil*

Apple Fritters with Calvados Butterscotch Sauce

1 Heat the sunflower oil in a deep-fat fryer to 190°C. TO MAKE THE SAUCE: Melt the butter in a saucepan and add the sugar, golden syrup and 2 tablespoons water. Place the pan over a gentle heat, stirring until the sugar dissolves. Increase the heat and boil the sauce rapidly for a few minutes until it turns pale golden in colour and thickens slightly.

2 Remove the pan from the heat and carefully pour in the cream – it might splatter. Stir until the cream mixes into the sauce, then return the pan to the heat and simmer until it reaches the desired consistency. Stir in the Calvados and simmer for 1-2 more minutes. Keep the sauce warm while you cook the fritters.

3 TO MAKE THE BATTER: Sift the flour, caster sugar and cinnamon into a bowl, then beat in the egg yolk and 8 tablespoons water to give a smooth batter. Whisk the egg white until stiff and fold it into the batter. Dip the apple slices in the batter and shake off any excess, then place in the hot oil.

4 Fry the fritters for 2-3 minutes on each side, until the batter is golden, and cooking 3-4 apple rings at a time.

5 Remove from the pan and drain the slices on absorbent kitchen paper. Keep them warm until all the apple slices are cooked. Serve the fritters hot with the sauce drizzled over them.

Greek Fig Tart

Serves 10
Calories: 266
Fat: 17g
Saturated fat: 10g
Suitable for freezing: ✗

- 100g (3½oz) unsalted butter
- 100g (3½oz) clear honey
  (or dark muscovado sugar)
- 2 tablespoons lime or
  lemon juice (or brandy)
- Good pinch of sea salt flakes
- 10-12 fresh figs,
  halved lengthways
- 375g butter-puff pastry
  block, defrosted if frozen
  (or 320g pack ready-rolled
  sweet shortcrust pastry)
- Greek yogurt or crème fraîche,
  to serve

- *20cm (8in) ovenproof frying
  pan or 23cm (9in) cake tin
  (not loose-based)*

1 Melt the butter with the honey (or sugar) in the frying pan over a medium heat. Let the mixture bubble to caramelise. Carefully stir in the lime or lemon juice (or brandy) and salt (it will spit).

2 Take the pan off the heat while you pack in the fig halves, cut side down. Put the pan back on the heat for 3 minutes, until the figs start to soften, then leave to cool for 15 minutes.

3 Set the oven to 200°C or Gas Mark 6. (If using a cake tin, transfer the hot caramel and figs to the tin.)Roll the pastry out so it's just large enough for you to cut out a round 2.5cm (1in) larger than the top of the pan, or the cake tin. Use a plate as a guide. Lay the pastry over the figs, tucking the excess inside the pan or tin.

4 Bake for 30-35 minutes (or 25-30 minutes if using shortcrust) until the pastry is crisp and golden. Run a knife around the pastry edge. Leave the pan or tin to cool on a rack for 20 minutes.

5 Put a large plate on top of the tart and flip it over to turn it out. Serve warm with dollops of Greek yogurt or crème fraîche.

TIP

This tart can be made
a few hours before
serving, turned out, and
warmed later, covered
loosely in foil, in
a medium oven for
10-15 minutes

Serves 5

Calories: 400

Fat: 10.5g

Saturated fat: 6.5g

Suitable for freezing: ✗

- 3 Bramley apples (about 500g/1lb) peeled, cut into wedges and cored
- 2 pears, peeled, cored and sliced
- 60g (2oz) caster sugar
- 1 level tablespoon cornflour
- ½ level teaspoon mixed spice

FOR THE COBBLER:
- 150g (5oz) self-raising flour
- 60g (2oz) butter, chilled
- 100g (3½oz) golden caster sugar
- 100ml (3½fl oz) buttermilk
- 1 level tablespoon golden granulated sugar

- *1.25 litre (2 pint) ovenproof dish, buttered*

Apple and Pear Cobbler

1 Set the oven to 200°C or Gas Mark 6. Put the prepared apples and pears into the dish. Sprinkle with the caster sugar, cornflour and mixed spice, and gently mix together.

2 TO MAKE THE COBBLER: Put the flour into a food processor with small chunks of butter and pulse for a few seconds to form crumbs. Add the sugar and buttermilk and whizz briefly to make a soft dough.

3 Pull off clumps of the dough and put them on the fruit— don't cover it completely. Sprinkle with granulated sugar and bake for 35-40 minutes, until the fruit is tender and the cobbler golden.

Steamed Meringues with Caramel Sauce

Serves 4

Calories: 283

Fat: 0g

Sat fat: 0g

Suitable for freezing: ✗

FOR THE MERINGUES;
- 125g (4oz) caster sugar
- 2 large egg whites

FOR THE CARAMEL SAUCE:
- 125g (4oz) granulated sugar
- Fresh pineapple, thinly sliced, to serve

- *4 x 2¾in cooking rings, lightly oiled on a lightly oiled flat plate*
- *A basin to fit over the meringues on the plate*

1 TO MAKE THE MERINGUES: Measure 90g (3oz) of the caster sugar into a small pan, add 3 tablespoons water and heat gently, stirring occasionally, to dissolve the sugar.

2 Bring the syrup to the boil, then to a temperature of 112-116°C on a sugar thermometer (soft ball stage) or it's ready when the syrup is thick but still clear and if you drop a little into a bowl of cold water it should form a ball.

3 Meanwhile, whisk the egg whites to a foam, then whisk in the rest of the sugar to form soft peaks.

4 Cool the hot pan quickly by immersing the base in a bowl of cold then, before the syrup sets in the pan, quickly pour it into the meringue mixture in a steady stream, with the electric hand mixer going at slow speed, if you can.

5 To steam the meringues, have a large pan of water ready with the water just moving, not fast boiling. Put the rings on the plate and spoon meringue mixture into each ring, swirling the top. Put the plate on the steamer and put an upturned mixing bowl over the top to keep the heat in. Steam gently for 5-7 minutes, until the meringue is just set.

6 Remove the bowl and plate from the steamer with care. Slide the meringues onto a plate or individual plates and lift off the cutters. While the meringues are cooking, make the sauce.

7 TO MAKE THE CARAMEL SAUCE: Put the sugar and 4 tablespoons water in a pan and let the sugar dissolve over a low heat, then bring to the boil and let it turn a deep golden. Take off the heat and, with care, pour about a quarter of the caramel onto a sheet of bakewell paper on a cold surface and leave to set.

8 Add 100ml (3½fl oz) water to the rest of the caramel in the pan. Watch, as it will spit. Put back on a low heat and let the caramel dissolve again, leave to cool a little. Drizzle some caramel sauce over the meringues. Serve the warm meringues with the pineapple or other fresh fruit. Decorate with shards of smashed caramel.

> **TIP**
>
> If the syrup does set before adding it to the meringue, gently reheat it to loosen it

Serves 8

Calories: 318	
Fat: 15g	
Saturated fat: 7g	
Suitable for freezing: ✗	

FOR THE PASTRY
- 45g (1½oz) whole, unblanched almonds
- 200g (7oz) plain flour
- ½ level teaspoon baking powder
- 1 level teaspoon ground cinnamon
- 90g (3oz) golden caster sugar
- 100g (3½oz) unsalted butter
- 1 medium egg
- Zest of ½ a lemon

FOR THE FILLING:
- 300g (10oz) frozen raspberries
- 60g (2oz) caster sugar, plus extra
- Zest and juice of ½ a lemon
- 300g (10oz) fresh raspberries
- 1 rounded teaspoon cornflour
- Crème fraîche, to serve

- *34 x 11cm (13½ x 4½in) baking tin*

TIP

Instead of the fresh fruit, try using 250g (4oz) cherry, raspberry or blackcurrant jam and 2 tablespoons of kirsch

Linzer Torte

1 TO MAKE THE PASTRY: Put the almonds in a food processor and whizz until chopped. Add the flour, baking powder, cinnamon and caster sugar, and whizz until just mixed. Add slivers of butter and whizz to breadcrumb stage, then add the egg and lemon zest, and whizz to a soft dough. Knead lightly and roll to form a long cylinder. Wrap in cling film and chill for 30 minutes.

2 TO MAKE THE FILLING: Put the frozen raspberries in a pan with the sugar. Heat gently until the sugar dissolves. Bring to the boil, then simmer for 20-25 minutes, until most of the liquid has evaporated. Stir occasionally. Add some lemon juice, pour into a bowl and cool.

3 Cut off 125g (4oz) of the pastry. Set aside for the lattice. Cut the rest of the pastry into fine discs and arrange on the base and sides of the tin. As they soften, press them to meld them together and line the tin. Trim excess from the top edge. Chill the pastry case and excess pastry while the oven heats up.

4 Set the oven to 190°C or Gas Mark 5. Place a baking sheet in the oven to heat up.

5 Spread the homemade jam in the pastry case. Toss the fresh raspberries with the cornflour and 1 teaspoon sugar and the lemon zest, and spread them evenly over the jam.

6 Roll out the reserved pastry and cut it into crinkle-edged strips, about 1.5cm (just over ½in) wide, cutting them to fit across the pie and form a lattice. Press ends onto the top, to seal.

7 Put the pie onto the hot baking sheet, place it near the bottom of the oven and bake for 25 minutes, then a further 15 minutes nearer the top. Take the pie out of oven and sprinkle with a little caster sugar. Leave it in the tin to set for 30 minutes, or longer. Serve at room temperature with dollops of crème fraîche.

Serves 4-6
Calories: 535
Fat: 38g
Saturated fat: 25g
Suitable for freezing: ✗

- 500g carton mascarpone cheese
- 90g (3oz) caster sugar
- 30g (1oz) dark chocolate, finely grated
- 2-3 level teaspoons instant coffee granules
- 100ml (3½fl oz) Tia Maria
- 24-30 amaretti biscuits, plus 4-6 biscuits, to decorate

TIP

For an extra-chocolatey taste, dust with a little cocoa powder

Tiramisu

1. Beat the mascarpone cheese until softened, then beat in the sugar. Reserve 1 tablespoon grated chocolate and beat in the rest.

2. Dissolve the coffee in 1 tablespoon boiling water and stir in the Tia Maria. Pour the coffee mixture over the amaretti biscuits on a deep plate and leave to soak for 1 minute. Put a soaked biscuit at the bottom of each glass. Add 1 teaspoon of the coffee liquid to each one, reserving the rest of the liquid for later.

3. Divide half the mascarpone mixture between the glasses, then top with the remaining soaked amaretti biscuits. Spoon on the rest of the mascarpone and pour the remaining coffee mixture over it.

4. Decorate with the extra amaretti biscuits and sprinkle over the reserved grated chocolate.

Florentine Eccles Cakes

Makes about 30

Calories: 106

Fat: 6g

Saturated fat: 4g

Suitable for freezing: ✔

- 60g (2oz) butter
- 125g (4oz) granulated sugar
- 150g (5oz) dried mixed fruit
- 50g (1¾oz) glacé cherries, chopped
- 50g (1¾oz) blanched almonds, chopped
- Finely zested rind 1 orange
- 1 level teaspoon ground cinnamon
- 375g packet all-butter puff pastry
- Milk, for glaze

- 10cm (4in) plain round cutter
- 2 baking sheets, lined with baking parchment

1 Set the oven to 220°C or Gas Mark 7
TO MAKE THE FILLING: Melt the butter. Reserve 1 level tablespoon granulated sugar and add the rest to the butter, and stir in the dried mixed fruit, glacé cherries, almonds, orange zest and cinnamon.

2 Roll out the puff pastry as thinly as possible and use the cutter to cut out rounds of pastry. Brush water around the edge of the pastry, then place 2 teaspoons of the filling in the centre of each. Gather up the edges to totally enclose the filling.

3 Roll out each little parcel to give a flat round, about 7cm (2¾in), where the fruit is just starting to show through the pastry. Make 3-4 slashes in the top of each cake, then place them on the lined baking sheets. Repeat to use up the pastry trimmings and until the filling is used up.

4 Brush the top of each cake with milk and sprinkle a little of the reserved sugar over each.

5 Bake in the centre of the oven for 15-20 minutes, swapping the position of the trays in the oven, if necessary, if the top ones are browning more quickly than the lower ones.

6 Remove the baking trays from the oven and transfer the cakes onto a wire rack to cool. Serve the eccles cakes warm or cold.
Note: These cakes are best eaten on the day that they are baked, but may be stored in an airtight container for up to 3 days.

❄ *Pack into a suitable freezer container, seal and label and freeze for up to 1 month. Reheat cakes in a hot oven for a few minutes before serving to refresh them*

Almond and Raspberry Crumble Squares

Makes 12

Calories: 360

Fat: 21g

Saturated: 9g

Suitable for freezing: ✗

- 250g (8oz) plain flour
- 100g (3½oz) ground almonds
- 100g (3½oz) caster sugar
- 200g (7oz) butter, chilled
- 200g (7oz) good raspberry jam
- 200g (7oz) fresh or frozen raspberries
- 60g (2oz) flaked almonds

- *18 x 28cm (7 x 11in) traybake tin, lined with baking parchment*

TIP

This is also good served warm as a pudding with custard

1 Set the oven to 180°C or Gas Mark 4. Put the flour, ground almonds and sugar in a food processor, add slivers of butter and whizz until the mixture just sticks together. Tip just under half the mixture (300g/10oz) into the tin and press evenly over the base until firm.

2 Spread the jam, then the raspberries, over the base. Sprinkle the rest of the mixture on top, then finish with the flaked almonds.

3 Bake for 50 minutes near the bottom of the oven until pale golden.

4 Cool in the tin, then cut into 12 squares and leave to go cold, then lift out of the tin to serve.

Makes about 12-15

Calories: 247

Fat: 19g

Saturated fat: 12g

Suitable for freezing: ✔

FOR THE CHOUX PASTRY:
- 60g (2oz) butter
- 75g (2½oz) plain flour
- 2 medium eggs

FOR THE FILLING:
- 200g bar dark chocolate
- 284ml carton whipping cream
- A few drops of vanilla extract

FOR THE TOPPING:
- 100g bar dark chocolate
- 30g (1oz) butter

- *Large piping bag fitted with a 1.5cm (¾in) plain piping tube*
- *Large star piping tube*
- *Baking sheets, lined with baking parchment*

Chocolate Eclairs

1 Set the oven to 220°C or Gas Mark 7.
TO MAKE THE CHOUX PASTRY: Place the butter in a saucepan and pour in 150ml (¼ pint) water. Place the pan over a medium heat until the butter melts. Increase the heat and bring the mixture to the boil. Remove the pan from the heat and quickly tip in the flour and beat the mixture until it binds together and comes away from the sides of the pan to form a ball. Leave the mixture to cool for at least 10 minutes, then beat in the eggs, one at a time.

2 Fill the piping bag fitted the plain piping tube. Pipe out lines of the choux pastry, about 7-8cm (3-3½in) long, on the lined baking sheets. Sprinkle some cold water over them, then bake them in the centre of the oven for 15-20 minutes, swapping the position of the trays if the ones on the top start to brown quicker than the lower ones.

3 Remove the trays with the éclairs from the oven and pierce each one with a skewer to allow steam to escape, then return the éclairs to the oven for a further 5-7 minutes, or until they are crisp. Remove the trays from the oven and transfer the éclairs to a wire rack and leave to cool completely.

4 Cut one side of each éclair in half and scoop out any soft mixture in the centres using a teaspoon.

5 TO MAKE THE FILLING: Break the chocolate into pieces and place it into a bowl. Pour the cream into a saucepan and bring it to the boil, then pour it over the chocolate. Stir until the chocolate dissolves and add vanilla extract to taste. Allow the mixture to cool, then chill it until it's thick.

6 Whisk the chocolate filling until it's light and fluffy and will hold its shape, then fill the piping bag fitted with the star piping tube with the mixture. Pipe some of the chocolate mixture into each éclair, then press the éclairs lightly to close them.

7 TO MAKE THE TOPPING: Place the chocolate and butter in a bowl and melt, either in a microwave oven, or over a pan of hot water. Dip the top of the éclairs into the mixture, taking care not to get any of the topping in the filling. This may be easier to do if it's brushed on with a pastry brush. Leave the topping to set before serving.

❀ *Pastry only is suitable for freezing. The unfilled choux fingers may be frozen, if wrapped in a freezer bag and sealed, for up to 3 months. Refresh them in a hot oven to crisp them up after defrosting, then leave them to cool before filling. They are not suitable for freezing with the filling and topping*

Makes 12

Calories: 200

Fat: 2.5g

Saturated fat: 1.5g

Suitable for freezing: ✗

FOR THE PAPER CASES:
- 30g (1oz) butter, melted

FOR THE DOUGH:
- 500g (1lb) strong plain flour
- 7g sachet fast action yeast
- ½ level teaspoon salt

FOR THE FILLING:
- 2 medium apples, peeled, cored and chopped
- 1 lemon, grated rind and juice
- 4 level tablespoons caster sugar
- 1 level tablespoon cinnamon

FOR THE ICING:
- 60-90g (2-3oz) icing sugar

- *12-hole muffin tray, lined with paper cases*
- *Small disposable piping bag*

TIP

If you don't like piping, then the glaze may be brushed over the top of the cobblestones

Apple and Cinnamon Cobblestones

1 Brush the inside of the paper muffin cases lightly with the melted butter.

2 TO MAKE THE DOUGH: Tip the flour into a bowl and stir in the yeast and salt. Add 350ml (12fl oz) lukewarm water. Mix the ingredients together to form a dough.

3 Knead the dough on a lightly floured surface for about 10 minutes until it's smooth and elastic. Put the dough in a bowl and cover with an oiled piece of cling film while you prepare the filling, so the dough doesn't form a crust.

4 TO PREPARE THE FILLING: Mix together the apples with the lemon rind and juice. In a large bowl, mix together the caster sugar and cinnamon.

5 Roll out the dough into a large rectangle to about 2cm (¾in) thickness. Use a pizza wheel or large knife to cut the dough into small cubes. Coat the cubes, a few at a time, in the sugar and cinnamon mixture. Place a few of the sugar-coated cubes in

each paper case. Add some apple, then some more cubes. Repeat the layering process until all the dough and apple has been used. Cover the tray with a sheet of oiled cling film and leave the mixture until it's doubled in size.

6 Set the oven to 220°C or Gas Mark 7. Bake the cobblestones in the centre of the oven for 15-20 minutes, or until they are golden in colour and sound hollow when tapped.

7 While the cobblestones are baking, mix together the icing sugar with 2-3 tablespoons water to give a runny glaze. Cover the bowl with a damp cloth so the icing doesn't start to dry out and form a crust.

8 Remove the cobblestones from the oven and transfer to a wire rack. Transfer the icing to the piping bag. Cut off the end of the piping bag to give a small hole and drizzle the icing over the top of the hot cobblestones. Leave the icing to set before serving. They may be served warm or cold.

Zesty Lemon Madeira Cake

Serves 6-8
Calories: 388
Fat: 21g
Saturated fat: 11g
Suitable for freezing: ✔

- 175g (6oz) butter, softened
- 175g (6oz) caster sugar
- 3 medium eggs
- 250g (8oz) self-raising flour
- Finely grated zest and juice of 1 lemon
- 2-3 thin slices citron peel, optional

- *18cm (7in) round cake tin, lined with baking parchment*

1 Set the oven to 180°C or Gas Mark 4. Cream together the butter and sugar until pale and fluffy, then beat in the eggs, one at a time, adding a spoonful of flour with each egg. Fold in the lemon zest and juice, then the remaining flour. Turn the mixture into the lined tin and level the surface.

2 Bake the cake in the centre of the oven for 25 minutes, then place the citron peel slices on the top of the cake, if using. Continue cooking the cake for a further 40-50 minutes, or until the cake is just firm to the touch in the centre and a skewer comes out clean after being inserted into the cake.

3 Remove the cake from the oven and leave to cool in the tin for 10-15 minutes, then transfer to a wire rack to cool completely.

❋ *Wrap the cake in a freezer bag and freeze for up to 3 months. Allow the cake to defrost before serving*

STARTERS

MAIN MEALS

DESSERTS

TEATIME TREATS

WINTER

Twice-baked Smoked Salmon Soufflé with Horseradish Cream

Serves 6-8

Calories: 261

Fat: 20g

Saturated fat: 11g

Suitable for freezing: ✗

- 50g (1¾oz) butter
- 50g (1¾oz) plain flour
- 300ml (½ pint) milk
- 100g (3½oz) full-fat cream cheese
- 1 level tablespoon chopped fresh dill
- 200g packet smoked salmon
- 3 large eggs, separated
- Zest of ½a lemon
- Freshly ground black pepper

TO SERVE:

- 1-2 tablespoons horseradish sauce
- 3 tablespoons crème fraîche
- Sprigs of dill
- Lemon slices, quartered
- Caviar or fish roe
- Salad leaves
- Olive oil, for drizzling

- 6-8 ramekin dishes, well buttered and base-lined with baking parchment

1 Set the oven to 180°C or Gas Mark 4. Melt the butter in a pan and add the flour, then gradually add the milk, beating well between each addition to give a smooth sauce. Simmer the sauce for a few minutes, then remove the pan from the heat and stir in the cream cheese and dill.

2 Cut 6-8 narrow strips of smoked salmon, long enough to wrap around the ramekin dishes, and reserve them, then chop the rest of it.

3 Whisk the egg whites until stiff. Beat the egg yolks, one at a time, into the sauce, then fold in the egg whites, chopped salmon, lemon zest and freshly ground black pepper.

4 Place the ramekin dishes in a roasting dish and pour boiling water around them, to come about halfway up the sides of the ramekins. Bake in the centre of the oven for about 15-20 minutes, until the soufflés have puffed up and just set.

5 Remove the soufflés from the oven and leave to cool for a few minutes. Turn them out onto a board, or plate, and leave to cool.

6 Spread some horseradish sauce over one side of the smoked salmon strips and wrap one around each soufflé, with the horseradish sticking them to the soufflés.

7 Set the oven to 190°C or Gas Mark 5. Place the soufflés on a baking sheet lined with baking parchment and bake in the oven for 12-15 minutes, or until they start to puff up.

8 Meanwhile, stir the remaining horseradish sauce into the crème fraîche.

9 Remove the soufflés from the oven and serve each with some horseradish cream spooned on top and garnished with a sprig of dill, a quartered slice of lemon and a little caviar or fish roe. Serve immediately with salad leaves, drizzled with olive oil.

> **TIP**
>
> The soufflés can be prepared a day in advance up to the end of Step 7

Cavelo, Prawn and Chorizo Stir-fry

Serves 2-3

Calories: 270

Fat: 17g

Saturated fat: 5g

Suitable for freezing: ✗

- 1 tablespoon flaked almonds
- 1 tablespoon olive oil
- 120g packet ready-diced chorizo
- 200g (7oz) raw, peeled Indonesian prawns
- About 100g (3½oz) Cavelo nero, cut into strips, or ready-shredded curly kale
- 1 red and 1 yellow pepper, grilled and skinned (use ready roasted for speed, if you prefer), cut into strips
- Salt and freshly ground black pepper
- Balsamic vinegar
- Chunks of rustic bread, to serve

1 Heat a wok or frying pan, add the nuts and cook them over a medium heat for 1-2 minutes to brown. Tip out and set aside.

2 Put the oil and chorizo in the pan and cook over a gentle heat for a minute, then turn up the heat, add the prawns and fry for 1-2 minutes on each side until lightly pink all over.

3 Take them out with a draining spoon. Reheat the oil left in the pan, add the Cavelo nero or kale and pepper strips and stir-fry for 2-3 minutes. Put the prawns and chorizo back in the pan and heat through. Season with salt and freshly ground black pepper, sprinkle with almonds and balsamic vinegar. Serve stir-fry with bread.

Makes 8-10

Calories: 137

Fat: 11g

Saturated fat 1g

Suitable for freezing: ✔

- 6 level tablespoons plain flour
- 1 level teaspoon turmeric
- 1 level teaspoon ground cumin
- 1 level teaspoon garam masala
- Salt and freshly ground black pepper
- 2 medium onions, peeled and sliced
- Raita (minty yogurt), to serve, optional

- *Deep-frying pan, with oil*

Onion Bhaji

1. Heat the oil in the deep-frying pan to 190°C. Mix the flour, spices and salt together in a bowl and add 3-4 tablespoons water, to make a stiff batter. Stir the onions into the batter, to coat.

2. Add a dessertspoon of the onion mixture to the pan. When it rises to the surface, add the next spoonful. Continue doing this until the pan is full. Cook for 3-4 minutes until the bhajis are cooked, turning them over halfway through. Remove from the pan and drain them on absorbent kitchen paper.

3. Cook the remainder of the onion mixture. The bhajis may be served immediately or reheated on a baking sheet in a hot oven for a few minutes. Serve with Raita, if you like.

※ *Pack the cooled bhajis in a plastic container and freeze for up to 1 month. Allow to defrost, then heat through in a hot oven before serving*

TIP

May be served with mango chutney instead of Raita

Serves 4

Calories: 561	
Fat: 35g	
Saturated fat: 8.5g	
Suitable for freezing: ✔	

- 3 red peppers, quartered and cored
- ½-1 red chilli, deseeded
- 1 red onion, peeled and cut into wedges
- 2 cloves garlic, peeled and left whole
- A few sprigs of thyme
- 2 tablespoons olive oil
- 400g can chopped tomatoes
- 600ml (1 pint) hot vegetable stock
- Salt and freshly ground black pepper

FOR THE CROUTES:

- 30g (1oz) each fresh parsley and chives
- 2 cloves garlic, peeled and crushed
- 1 tablespoon toasted pine nuts
- 30g (1oz) Parmesan, grated
- 6 tablespoons olive oil
- 60g (2oz) mature Cheddar, grated
- 1 small ciabatta loaf, cut into 12 slices

Red Pepper and Tomato Soup with Pesto Croutes

1 Set the grill to medium. Put the peppers and chilli, skin-side up, with the onion, garlic and thyme on a sturdy baking tray. Mix in the oil and put the tray under the grill until the skin on the peppers blisters and browns, about 10-12 minutes. Turn the onion wedges halfway through cooking. Cool for a few minutes, then peel the skin off the peppers and chilli.

2 Tip the vegetables into a large pan, scraping in the juices as well. Add the can of tomatoes and the hot stock. Bring to the boil and simmer for 10 minutes. Whizz with a stick blender, then season. Pour into a jug, then into hot mugs or bowls.

3 TO MAKE THE PESTO CROUTES: Put all the ingredients, except the Cheddar and bread, in a tall jug and season. Whizz with a stick blender to make a chunky sauce. Add 4 tablespoons of this pesto to the grated Cheddar.

4 Toast the bread lightly on both sides, then spread one side with the cheesy pesto mixture. Put under the grill until the cheese melts. Serve the soup with the extra pesto, if you like, and the croutes.

❋ *May be frozen for up to 1 month. Allow to defrost before reheating thoroughly*

Three Cheese Roulade

Serves 10-12

Calories: 364

Fat: 28

Saturated fat: 13g

Suitable for freezing: ✗

- 75g (2½oz) butter
- 100g (3½oz) plain flour
- 500ml (16fl oz) milk
- 6 large eggs, separated
- Salt and freshly ground black pepper
- 90g (3oz) freshly grated Parmesan or pecorino
- 250g carton ricotta cheese
- 200g soft goat's cheese, crumbled
- About 25g (¾oz) fresh parsley, chopped
- 150-200g (5-7oz) ready-roasted peppers, drained and roughly chopped

TO SERVE:
- 6 tablespoons grated Parmesan
- 145g carton fresh pesto

- *38 x 25cm (15 x 10in) Swiss roll tin, lined with baking parchment*

1 Set the oven to 180°C or Gas Mark 4. Melt the butter gently in a pan, add the flour and stir for 1-2 minutes, until smooth. Add the milk and whisk well until thickened. Add the egg yolks, one at a time, beating until smooth. Take off the heat and season well with salt and freshly ground black pepper.

2 Whisk the egg whites with a pinch of salt in a large bowl to stiff peaks. Fold a third of them into the sauce, then add the mixture to the rest of the whites in the bowl and fold them in.

3 Spread the mix into the tin, sprinkle with a third of the Parmesan and bake for 20-25 minutes, until golden. Turn out onto parchment. Leave to cool.

4 Mix the ricotta and goat's cheese with the rest of the Parmesan and the parsley. Season with salt and freshly ground black pepper. Spread over the roulade. Scatter over the peppers. Using the paper as a guide, roll up the roulade from one of the long sides, finishing seam down. Wrap tightly in cling film. Chill for at least 2 hours.

5 To serve, set the oven to 220°C or Gas Mark 7 and line a baking tray with baking parchment. Trim the ends of the roulade, then cut into 10 or 12 thick slices. Place the slices on the tray and sprinkle with Parmesan. Warm through for 10 minutes, until the cheese starts to melt. Serve with pesto and salad.

**Serves 4 as a starter
or 2 as a light meal**

Calories: 162

Fat: 12g

Saturated fat: 4.5

Suitable for freezing: ✗

- 4 figs
- 60-90g (2-3oz) Gorgonzola, crumbled
- 2 slices Parma ham
- Small bag rocket salad

FOR THE DRESSING:
- 3 tablespoons olive oil
- 1 tablespoon balsamic vinegar
- 1 level tablespoon clear honey
- 1 level teaspoon Dijon mustard
- Salt and freshly ground black pepper

Parma-wrapped Gorgonzola Figs

1 Set the oven to 200°C or Gas Mark 6. Cut a cross in the top of each fig and fill with the crumbled Gorgonzola. Cut the slices of Parma ham in half lengthways and wrap one piece around each fig. Put the figs on a small baking sheet and place them in the centre of the oven. Cook for 5-10 minutes, until the cheese starts to melt.

2 Meanwhile, TO MAKE THE DRESSNG: Whisk all the ingredients together.

3 Divide the salad leaves between either 2 or 4 plates and put either 1 or 2 figs on the plates. Drizzle the dressing over the salad, plus a little over the figs, if you like. Season with freshly ground black pepper. Serve straight away.

Old-fashioned Pea and Ham Soup

Serves 8
Makes about 2 litres (3½ pints)
Calories: 244
Fat: 6g
Saturated fat: 2g
Suitable for freezing: ✔

- 300g (10oz) dried yellow
  split peas
- 1 litre (1¾ pints) chicken or
  vegetable stock, or water
- 2 onions, peeled and quartered
- 2 carrots, peeled and
  cut into big chunks
- 2 celery sticks, chopped
- 2 bay leaves and a few
  sprigs of fresh thyme
- 500g (1lb) joint of
  smoked gammon
- Salt and freshly ground
  black pepper
- Chopped parsley, to garnish

1 Rinse the dried yellow split peas thoroughly and put them in a large bowl. Cover with cold water and set aside, covered, overnight.

2 Drain peas and put in a big stockpot. Pour in the stock, or water, bring to the boil and boil for 10 minutes. Add the onion, carrot, celery, herbs and gammon. Bring back to the boil, skim off any scum, then reduce the heat to very low. Cover and simmer for 1½ hours.

3 Take out the gammon. Set aside to cool a little. Remove the bay leaves and sprigs of thyme. Blend the peas, vegetables and stock in a food processor until smooth. Put back into the pan and heat through for serving, adjusting the consistency and checking for seasoning.

4 Remove the skin and fat from the gammon and shred the meat (you should have about 350g/12oz) into small pieces. Serve the hot soup with chunks of meat added, and garnish with parsley.

✳ *May be frozen for up to 1 month. Allow to defrost before reheating thoroughly*

White Nut Timbales

Makes 6

Calories: 400

Fat: 27g

Saturated fat: 9g

Suitable for freezing: ✔

- 45g (1½oz) butter
- 1 red onion, peed and finely chopped
- 1 clove garlic, peeled and crushed
- 100g (3½oz) pine nuts, finely chopped
- 125g (4oz) white breadcrumbs
- 1 lemon
- 60g (2oz) smoked Cheddar cheese, grated
- 280g jar (170g drained weight) sliced artichokes in olive oil, drained and chopped
- 200g (7oz) ready-cooked and peeled chestnuts, all but 3 chopped
- Salt and freshly ground black pepper
- 1 medium egg, lightly beaten
- 2 tablespoons each of chopped fresh parsley, sage and thyme
- 6 sage leaves

- *Baking tray, lined with a non-stick liner*
- *6 rings (7.5cm/3in) lined with baking parchment*

1 Heat the butter in a pan, add the onion and garlic and cook for 5 minutes.

2 Add the pine nuts, breadcrumbs, rind and juice of half the lemon, cheese, artichokes and chestnuts. Season, stir in egg and herbs.

3 Divide the mixture between the rings. Smooth the tops with a palette knife. Cut the remaining lemon half into slices. Arrange half a lemon slice, half a chestnut and 1 sage leaf on top of each. Cover and chill until needed.

4 Set the oven to 200°C or Gas Mark 6. Bake timbales for 15 minutes or until golden.

❋ *Open-freeze, unbaked, on a tray. Bake as above from frozen for 20 minutes*

Minted Lamb Cobbler

Serves 3-4

Calories: 822

Fat: 40g

Saturated fat: 15g

Suitable for freezing: ✔

- 3 tablespoons olive oil
- 6 rasher smoked streaky bacon, chopped
- 250g (8oz) shallots, peeled
- 350g (12oz) Chantenay carrots or baby carrots
- 2 parsnips, peeled and chopped
- 400-500g (14oz-1lb) diced lamb
- 2 tablespoons plain flour
- 300ml (½ pint) red wine
- 1 lamb stock cube
- 1 tablespoon chopped fresh mint
- 1 teaspoon Marmite
- Salt and freshly ground black pepper

FOR THE TOPPING:
- 250g (8oz) self-raising flour
- 50g (1¾oz) butter
- 2 level tablespoons
- 1 medium egg
- About 100ml (3½fl oz) milk

- *1.75 litre (3 pint) casserole dish*
- *6.5cm (2¾in) plain round cutter*

1 Set the oven to 180°C or Gas Mark 4. Heat 1 tablespoon olive oil in a sauté pan and add the bacon and shallots. Cook over a medium heat for 5-7 minutes, until they start to brown. Add the carrots and parsnips to the pan, and cook for a further 3-4 minutes.

2 Tip the contents of the pan into the casserole dish. Return the pan to the heat and add the remaining oil. When the oil is very hot, add the meat to the pan. Cook the meat over a high heat for 4-5 minutes, turning it occasionally to brown the surface, taking care not to turn it too much, as the meat will brown better if left to do it on each surface rather than continually turning it. Sprinkle the flour over the meat and stir to coat it. Pour in the red wine, stir well, and bring to the boil and simmer for a few minutes. Pour in 300ml (½ pint) water and crumble in the stock cube. Add the mint, Marmite and seasoning. Pour the mixture into the casserole. Cover the dish, either with a lid or foil, and cook in the centre of the oven for 1½-1¾ hours.

3 TO MAKE THE SCONES FOR THE TOPPING: Tip the flour into a bowl and rub in the butter. Stir in the mint and season with salt and freshly ground black pepper. Beat the egg with enough milk to make it up to 150ml (¼ pint). Reserve about 2 tablespoons of the egg mixture and pour the rest into the flour. Use a round-bladed knife to mix the ingredients into a dough. Turn the dough out on to the work surface and knead it very lightly to give a smooth surface.

4 Roll the dough out on a floured surface and cut out about 8 rounds, about 2.5cm (1in) thick, re-rolling the trimmings as necessary.

5 Working quickly, take the casserole out of the oven. Place the scones on top and brush with the reserved egg mixture, then return the dish to the oven, uncovered, for 20-30 minutes, or until the scones have risen. Serve immediately with mashed potatoes and steamed green vegetables.

❊ *The stew can be packed into a freezer container when cold and frozen for up to 1 month. Let it defrost before reheating and cooking with the scones. The scone topping is not suitable for freezing*

TIP

If you don't like Marmite, leave it out and add a good dash of Worcestershire sauce

Vegetable and Polenta Terrine

Serves 8

Calories: 285

Fat: 13g

Saturated fat: 6g

Suitable for freezing: ✗

- 2 tablespoons olive oil
- 2 courgettes, trimmed and sliced
- 2 red onions, peeled and sliced
- 2 red peppers, deseeded and sliced
- 250g (8oz) polenta
- Salt and freshly ground back pepper
- 2 cloves garlic, peeled and crushed
- 60g (2oz) butter
- 75g (2½oz) Parmesan, grated
- 198g can sweetcorn, drained
- 8 sun blush tomatoes in oil, drained
- 8 basil leaves

- *900g (2lb) loaf tin lined with baking parchment*

1 Set the oven to 220°C or Gas Mark 7. Put the oil, courgettes red onion and pepper into large roasting tin. Stir to coat in oil, then roast for 20 minutes until tender and beginning to char.

2 Put the polenta into a pan, add some salt, garlic and 1 litre (1¾ pints) boiling water. Heat and stir for a few minutes until thickened and coming away from the sides of the pan. Stir in the butter, Parmesan and sweetcorn. Season with freshly ground black pepper.

3 Arrange tomatoes and basil on the base of the loaf tin. Spoon over half of the warm polenta mixture and level surface. Arrange the rest of the roasted vegetables on top. Cover with the rest of the polenta, then arrange the rest of the roasted vegetables on top.

4 Cover with baking parchment and wrap in foil. Cool and chill for 4 hours, or overnight.

5 To serve: Set oven to 200°C or Gas Mark 6. Warm in the oven for 25 minutes. Turn out and slice.

TIP

Look out for instant polenta (find it in supermarkets). It thickens in a couple of minutes when heated

Serves 3-4

Calories: 440

Fat: 27g

Saturated fat: 9g

Suitable for freezing: ✔

- 2 tablespoons sunflower oil
- 6-8 sausages – Toulouse or chorizo style
- 1 onion, peeled and cut into thin wedges
- 4 sticks celery, sliced
- 125g (4oz) chestnut mushrooms, sliced
- 400g can chopped tomatoes
- 2 ham or pork stock cubes
- 125g (4oz) flageolet beans, soaked overnight

- *1.25 litres (2 pint) casserole dish or slow-cook pot*

Sausage and Bean Stew

1 If cooking in the oven, set the oven to 180°C or Gas Mark 4. Heat half of the oil in a frying pan and add the sausages. Fry them for 7-10 minutes over a medium heat, turningthem occasionally, until they're browned, then remove from the pan and place in the casserole dish or slow-cook pot.

2 Add the remaining oil to the pan, then the onion and celery, and cook for about 5-7 minutes, stirring occasionally, until the vegetables start to soften. Add the mushrooms and cook for a further 2-3 minutes.

3 Tip the tomatoes into the pan and crumble in the stock cubes and add 300ml (½ pint) water. Add the drained beans. Bring the mixture to the boil and boil, uncovered, for 10 minutes.

4 Remove the pan from the heat and then pour the bean mixture over the sausages and cover the dish.

5 Either cook in the centre of the oven for 1½–1¾ hours, or in the slow-cook pot on Auto or Medium for 5-6 hours.

❊ *The cold stew may be packed into a suitable container and frozen for up to 1 month. Let it defrost before reheating*

Serves 12

Calories: 440

Fat: 29g

Saturated fat 15g

Suitable for freezing: ✗

- Salt and freshly ground black pepper
- 1-1.5kg (2¼-3lb) beef fillet
- 60g (2oz) butter
- 2 shallots, peeled and chopped
- 2 cloves garlic, peeled and crushed
- 250g (8oz) chestnut mushrooms, finely chopped
- 2 teaspoons chopped fresh thyme leaves
- 250g tub mascarpone cheese
- 2 tablespoons wholegrain mustard
- 2 x 80g packs Parma ham
- 375g packet ready-rolled puff pastry
- 1 medium egg, beaten

FOR THE SAUCE:
- 2 tablespoons olive oil
- 350g (12oz) shallots, peeled and chopped
- 2-3 cloves garlic, peeled and crushed
- 3 tablespoons tomato purée
- 2 tablespoons balsamic vinegar
- 200ml (7fl oz) red wine
- 300ml (½ pint) hot beef stock

Beef en Croute

1 Season the beef well. Heat 30g (1oz) butter in a large frying pan over a medium heat and, when foaming, put the fillet in pan and brown it all over for 4-5 minutes, taking care not to let the butter burn. Cool meat and cover.

2 Meanwhile, melt the rest of butter in the pan, add the chopped shallots and cook for 1 minute. Add the garlic, mushrooms and thyme and fry for a few minutes.

3 Bet the mascarpone with the mustard until smooth. Mix in the mushroom mixture. Season.

4 Lay half the Parma ham slices on a large piece of cling film with slices overlapping. Spread half the mushroom mixture on one side of the beef, then turn it over on top of the Parma ham. Spread the rest of the mushroom mixture over the top and sides of the beef, then wrap the rest of the Parma ham slices round, overlapping on top of the mushroom mixture. Wrap in cling film and chill in the fridge.

5 Heat the oven to 220°C or Gas Mark 7. Roll out the pastry and cut off a third. Roll out the smaller

piece to 5mm (¼in) thickness and 2.5cm (1in) bigger than the beef. Prick several times with a fork. Transfer to a baking sheet and bake for 12-15 minutes or until brown and crisp. Allow to cool for a few minutes, then trim to the size of the beef. Remove the cling film from the beef and place on the cooked pastry, brushing pastry edges with egg.

6 Roll out the rest of the pastry to a rectangle 25 x 30cm (10 x 12in). Cut 10 diagonal slashes in the pastry. Cover the beef with the pastry, tucking the ends under the cooked pastry base. Brush with the beaten egg. Cook a baking sheet for 40 minutes for rare to medium-rare; 45 minutes for medium. Leave to stand for 10 minutes before serving.

7 TO MAKE THE SAUCE: Heat the olive oil in a pan, and fry shallots until soft, about 10 minutes. Add garlic and tomato purée and cook for 1 minute, then add the balsamic vinegar. Bubble for 1 minute before adding red wine. Continue to boil for a few minutes to reduce, then add the beef stock and boil for 10 minutes more until reduced by a third. Serve with the beef.

Winter Root Vegetable Tagine

Serves 4

Calories: 353

Fat: 6.5g

Saturated fat: 0.8g

Suitable for freezing: ✗

- 1 tablespoon olive oil
- 2 onions, peeled and sliced
- 2 cloves garlic, peeled and crushed
- 2 tablespoons tomato purée
- 2 tablespoons harissa paste
- 4 carrots, peeled and halved lengthways
- 3 parsnips, peeled and halved lengthways
- 2 sweet potatoes, peeled and each cut into 4
- 300g (10oz) butternut squash, peeled, deseeded and cut into 2.5cm (1in) chunks
- 600ml (1 pint) hot vegetable stock
- Salt and freshly ground black pepper
- 400g can chickpeas, drained
- 400g can chopped tomatoes
- 2 tablespoons chopped fresh coriander leaves, to serve

- *2.5 litre (4 pint) flameproof casserole dish*

1 Heat the olive oil in the casserole dish and fry the onions for 5 minutes to soften but not brown.

2 Add the garlic, tomato purée and harissa paste and cook for 1 minute.

3 Add the carrots, parsnips, sweet potatoes and butternut squash. Pour in the stock and season with salt and freshly ground black pepper.

Cover and simmer for 25 minutes until the vegetables are tender. Stir in the chickpeas and canned tomatoes and warm through for 5 minutes. Serve sprinkled with fresh coriander.

✸ *When cold, pack into freezer container and freeze for up to 1 month. Allow to defrost before reheating*

TIP

You can add celeriac rather than parsnips, and use beans instead of chickpeas

Simple Lemon Chicken

Serves 6-8
Calories: 182
Fat: 4g
Saturated fat: 0.8g
Suitable for freezing: ✗

- 2 lemons
- 2 tablespoons olive oil
- Salt and freshly ground black pepper
- 1.75kg (3¾lb) chicken
- 1 large onion, peeled and finely sliced
- 1 head of fennel, trimmed and finely sliced
- 1 large leek, trimmed and sliced
- 6 sprigs of thyme or basil

1 Set the oven to 190°C or Gas Mark 5. Use a peeler to take the skin off the lemons. Cut half of the shavings into thin strips. Juice the lemons.

2 Heat the olive oil in a frying pan over a medium heat, season the chicken and brown it all over. Set it aside on a plate.

3 Add the onion to the pan and cook for 5 minutes, then add the fennel and leek and cook for another 5 minutes. Put the vegetables into a casserole or roasting tin, add the thyme or basil sprigs. Place the chicken on top, pour over the juice from the 2 lemons and sprinkle with the lemon strips and shavings.

4 Pour in 300ml (½ pint) hot water, cover with a lid or foil, and cook for 1½ hours. Take off the foil and continue cooking for 30-40 minutes more, or until juices run clear from the thigh when pierced with a skewer, and the vegetables are tender.

5 Leave for 10 minutes before serving, straight from the dish, spooning the vegetables and lemony juices over each portion of meat.

TIP

Eat any leftover meat cold, but heat leftover veg in their juices to serve with it

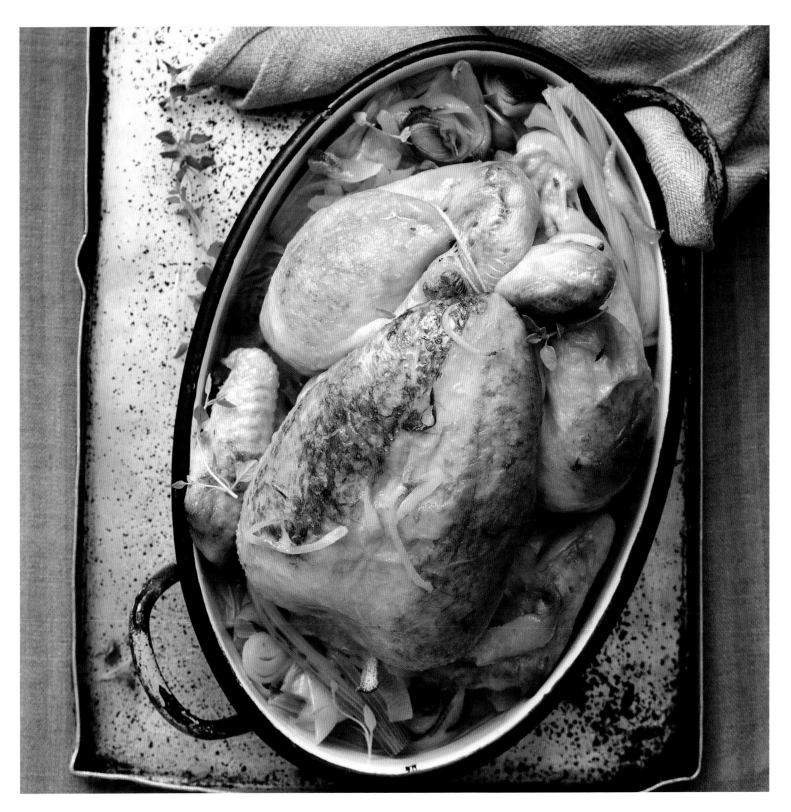

Cabbage Parcels

Serves 6
Calories: 266
Fat: 7g
Saturated fat: 2.5g
Suitable for freezing: ✗

- 12 leaves peeled off in turn from a large Savoy cabbage

FOR THE FILLING:
- 1 small onion, peeled and finely chopped
- 150g (5oz) each lean minced beef and minced pork
- 250g packet ready-cooked brown basmati rice
- 1 rounded teaspoon each of ground cumin, coriander and cinnamon
- Pinch of crushed dried chillies
- 2 tablespoons chopped fresh parsley
- Salt and freshly ground black pepper

FOR THE TOMATO SAUCE:
- 1 tablespoon olive oil
- 1 small onion, peeled and finely chopped
- 1 clove garlic, peeled and finely chopped
- Pinch of crushed dried chillies
- 400g can whole plum tomatoes

- *Shallow baking dish*

TIP

Use whichever minced meat you like, and white rice instead of brown. Toasted pine nuts are tasty added to the filling, too

1 TO MAKE THE TOMATO SAUCE: Heat the olive oil with the onion, garlic and dried chillies in a pan and cook, stirring occasionally, over a low to medium heat for about 5 minutes. Add the tomatoes, with their juice, and bash them down with a spoon. Simmer for about 15 minutes until thickened. Season. Whizz with a stick blender to make a chunky sauce. Set aside.

2 Meanwhile, TO MAKE THE FILLING: Put all the ingredients into a large bowl and mix together — using 2 forks is the easiest way.

3 Set the oven to 190°C or Gas Mark 5. Add the cabbage leaves (4 or 6 at a time) to a pan of boiling salted water and cook for 2 minutes until softened. Take them out with tongs and place in a colander and cool them under cold running water or put in a bowl of iced water. Cook the rest of the leaves in batches.

4 Pat the leaves dry in a tea towel and put them, underside up on the work surface and slice along the thick vein from the base, to make it thinner. Turn the leaves over.

5 Divide the stuffing mixture between them. Fold the stem end up over the filling, then fold in the sides and roll them up to make a parcel. Spoon a little of the tomato sauce and 3 tablespoons hot water, into a large, buttered shallow baking dish. Arrange the parcels, seam side down in the dish. Spoon the rest of the sauce over. Cover with Bakewell paper, then foil, or the lid, and bake for 1 hour.

Serves 6
Calories: 390
Fat: 17g
Saturated fat: 6g
Suitable for freezing: ✔

- 1 tablespoon olive oil
- 1 large onion, peeled and chopped
- 1 red chilli, deseeded and finely chopped
- 410g can black-eyed beans, and finely chopped
- 2 cloves garlic, peeled and finely chopped
- ½ teaspoon mild chilli powder, optional
- 410g can black-eyed beans, drained and rinsed
- 410g can red kidney beans, drained and rinsed
- 2 x 400g cans chopped tomatoes
- 1 tablespoon tomato ketchup
- Salt and freshly ground black pepper
- 12 taco shells (1 packet)

TO SERVE:
- About 6 tablespoons grated Cheddar cheese
- About 6 tablespoons sour cream
- A few coriander leaves
- 1 lime, cut into wedges

TIP

Blitz some of the mixture in the pan with a stick blender to thicken it more

Chilli Bean Tacos

1. Heat the olive oil in a large pan and cook the onion and chilli for 5 minutes until softened. Add the garlic and chilli powder, if using, and cook for another 5 minutes.

2. Add the beans and tomatoes and simmer for 20 minutes until thickened. Add the ketchup. Season.

3. Heat the taco shells in the oven for a few minutes, according to the pack instructions.

4. Fill the tacos with the bean mixture and serve with the grated Cheddar cheese and sour cream to spoon over, and coriander leaves to sprinkle on top. Serve the lime wedges on the side.

Luscious Apple Surprise Pie

Serves 8-10

Calories: 430

Fat: 18g

Saturated fat: 11g

Suitable for freezing: ✗

FOR THE PASTRY:

- 200g (7oz) butter
- 45g (1½oz) golden caster sugar (2 tablespoons)
- 2 medium eggs
- 300g (10oz) plain flour
- Pinch of salt

FOR THE FILLING:

- 100g (3½oz) golden caster sugar, plus 1-2 teaspoons for sprinkling
- ½-1 level teaspoon ground cinnamon or mixed spice
- 3 level tablespoons cornflour
- About 1.75kg (3½lb) cooking apples
- 3 tablespoons apricot conserve or good jam
- Custard or cream, to serve

- 1.75 litre (3 pint) capacity or a 25 x 5cm (10 x 2in) pie dish

1 TO MAKE THE PASTRY: Cut the butter into slivers into a food processor, add the sugar and whizz until just mixed. Add 1 whole egg and 1 egg yolk (keep the white for later) and whizz again, then add the flour and salt, and whizz until the mixture starts to come together. Gently work into a cylindrical shape. Take off just over a third of the pastry to use for the top of the pie. Form both pieces of pastry dough into flat rounds, wrap them in cling film and chill for about 45 minutes.

2 Set the oven to 190°C or Gas Mark 5 and put a baking sheet in the oven to heat up.

3 TO MAKE THF FILLING: Mix the sugar, spice and cornflour in a large bowl. Peel, core and cut the apples into thick slices — you should have at least 1kg (2¼lb) — adding them to the bowl.

4 Roll out the larger piece of pastry, on a lightly-floured surface and use it to line the pie dish. Trim it, but leave a little hanging over the edge. Lightly whisk the reserved egg white and brush the pastry case inside with some of it. Put the apple mixture into the pastry case, leaving a well in the middle. Spoon the apricot conserve or jam into the well

5 Add the pastry trimmings to the smaller piece of pastry and roll it out to form a lid. Dip your finger in water and pat it round the pastry rim. Lay the lid on top of the apple and press the edges together well to seal. Tuck any overhanging pastry under the rim of the dish. Press a fork around the edges and make a hole in the top. Brush the top with the rest of the egg white and sprinkle with 1-2 teaspoons sugar.

6 Put the pie on the baking sheet in the oven, to bake for 45 minutes. Allow to stand for 10 minutes before serving with hot custard or cream.

White Chocolate Parfait

Serves 6-8

Calories: 210

Fat: 16g

Saturated fat: 10g

Suitable for freezing: ✔

- 100g bar white chocolate, broken into squares
- 250ml (8fl oz) vanilla custard (ready-made) at room temperature
- 3 tablespoons Baileys Irish Cream liqueur
- 150ml carton double cream

TO SERVE:
- 2 tablespoons grated plain chocolate
- A few fresh raspberries

- *Small loaf tin lined with cling film*

1 Put the chocolate in a medium-sized bowl over a pan of simmering water. When it has melted, gradually stir in the custard until smooth.

2 Leave the mixture to cool at room temperature. Stir in the Baileys. Whip the cream and fold that in. Pour into the lined loaf tin.

❄ *Freeze until solid (overnight). Cover, seal and label. Use within 2 months.*

TO SERVE FROM THE FREEZER: Put in the fridge for about 20 minutes before serving. Turn out and decorate with grated chocolate and raspberries, then slice for serving and serve with extra fruit, if you like.

Makes 8

Calories: 292

Fat: 8g

Saturated fat: 3g

Suitable for freezing: ✗

- 270g packet (6 sheets) filo pastry
- 45g (1½oz) butter, melted
- 410g jar mincemeat
- 125g (4oz) fresh or frozen cranberries
- 2 teaspoons icing sugar, for dusting

- *8 x 7.5cm (3in) Yorkshire pudding tins, brushed with butter*

Cranberry and Mincemeat Filo Tarts

1 Set the oven to 200°C or Gas Mark 6. Cut the stack of filo pastry sheets into 10cm (4in) squares. Cover with cling film while you work with them.

2 Layer up 4 filo pastry squares in the base of a tin, brushing each layer with butter and arranging the pastry at alternate angles, like the points of a star. Repeat with the rest of the pastry to make 8 tarts. Bake for 10 minutes, until crisp and golden.

3 Spoon the mincemeat into the tarts and push the cranberries into each one. Bake for 5 minutes, until the cranberries soften slightly. Dust with icing sugar to serve.

Jasmine Rice Pudding

Serves 4

Calories: 274

Fat: 8g

Saturated fat: 4g

Suitable for freezing: ✗

- 600ml (1 pint) full cream or semi-skimmed milk
- 30g (1oz) caster sugar
- 60g (2oz) Thai Jasmine rice or pudding rice lime
- 1 tablespoon chopped pistachio nuts

FOR THE FRUIT BASE:

- 100g (3.oz) fresh or frozen cranberries
- 100ml (3½fl oz) cranberry juice drink
- 1 ripe apple or pear
- 2 pieces of stem ginger, chopped, and 2 tablespoons ginger syrup (from the jar of stem ginger)
- Knob of butter

- *4 small glasses, bowls or cups*

1 Pour the milk into a pan, add the sugar and rice. Cook over a medium heat for about 30 minutes, stirring every few minutes, until thickened and the rice is tender. Pour into a bowl, then grate in some lime zest and stir in the juice. Leave to cool.

2 TO MAKE THE FRUIT BASE: Simmer cranberries with the juice drink in a small pan for 5 minutes. Peel and chop the apple or pear, add to the pan and simmer for another 5 minutes, then stir in the chopped ginger, syrup and butter to make a thick sauce. Leave to cool.

3 Spoon the fruit into glasses, then top with the rice and sprinkle with the pistachios.

TIP

For even more Thai flavour, use a 400ml can of coconut milk, topped up with milk, and 1 teaspoon ground cardamom (the seeds from about 12 pods)

Passion Puddings

Makes 4 (recipe easily doubled)

Calories: 571

Fat: 38g

Saturated fat: 16g

Suitable for freezing: ✔

- 45g (1½oz) sultanas
- ½ orange, finely grated zest and juice
- 90g (3oz) self-raising wholemeal flour (or ½ wholemeal and ½ white self-raising flour)
- 90g (3oz) light soft brown sugar
- ½ teaspoon bicarbonate of soda
- ½ teaspoon ground cinnamon
- 1½ teaspoon mixed spice
- Pinch of salt
- 4 tablespoons sunflower oil
- 1 medium egg, beaten
- 90g (3oz) 1 medium carrot, peeled and finely grated
- 2 pineapple rings from a 227g can, chopped, set aside the other 2 slices and the juice
- 30g (1oz) pecans or walnuts, roughly chopped

FOR THE SAUCE:
- 1 orange, pared rind and juice
- 1 pot crème fraîche

- *4 dariole moulds, lightly buttered, base-lined*

1 Soak the sultanas in the orange rind and 2 tablespoons of the juice for an hour, if you have time.

2 Set the oven to 180°C or Gas Mark 4. Sift the flour into a large bowl and mix in the sugar, soda, spices and salt. Add the oil and egg and mix well, then fold in the grated carrot, chopped pineapple, nuts and sultanas with the juice.

3 Divide the mixture between the 4 dariole moulds. Put on a baking tray and bake for 30-35 minutes, until well-risen and just firm.

4 TO MAKE THE SAUCE: Pare the rind from about half the orange. Cut into very fine strips and blanch these in a pan of boiling water for 1 minute, then drain and rinse under cold water. Set aside.

5 Mix the juice from the orange and half orange leftover from the puddings, with the juice from the can of pineapple, in a small pan. Bring to the boil and boil for 5 minutes until reduced to about 4 tablespoons. Add the crème fraîche and boil for another 5 minutes.

6 Leave the puddings in tins for 5 minutes, then slip a palette round the edges and turn them out. Spoon a little sauce over and decorate with orange strips. Serve warm with the extra sauce.

✽ *Cool the puddings. Pack in a polybag, seal, label and freeze. Use within 3 months. Reheat in the microwave for a few minutes*

TIP

The sauce will thicken, then set firm as it cools. It can be made in advance and warmed through gently for serving

Sweet Wine Clementine Jelly

Serves 8

Calories: 79

No fat

Suitable for freezing: ✗

- 12 sheets leaf gelatine
- 375ml bottle Muscat
- About 850ml (1½ pints) juice from 20 clementines
- Physalis, to decorate, optional

- *1.25 litre (2 pint) jelly mould, wetted*

1 Soak the gelatine leaves in 4 tablespoons cold water for 10 minutes.

2 Gently heat the Muscat and strained clementine juice in a large pan over a medium/low heat until tepid. Stir in the soaked gelatine and keep stirring until it is completely dissolved. Strain into a jug and leave to cool.

3 Pour the mixture into the jelly mould. Chill and leave to set overnight.

4 Turn out by dipping the mould in hot water for few seconds. Decorate with physalis, if you like.

TIP

Metal jelly moulds will leave a more defining impression on the jelly, so search in the back of your cupboard, or in a charity shop, to find one! If you want to make the jelly just in a bowl or glasses, cut the amount of gelatine down to 10 leaves

Black Forest Trifle

Serves 8-10

Calories: 436

Fat: 29g

Saturated fat: 15g

Suitable for freezing: ✗

- 425g can of black cherries in syrup
- 250g chocolate finger cakes, or marble cake
- 4 tablespoons kirsch
- 100g bar plain chocolate
- 500g pot vanilla custard
- 300ml double cream
- 150ml single cream
- 1 tablespoon icing sugar
- ½ teaspoon vanilla extract

1 Drain the black cherries in a sieve over a bowl and reserve the juice.

2 Arrange half the sponge fingers in the base of a large trifle bowl, breaking them in half as you put them in. Spoon over 6 tablespoons of cherry juice and 3 tablespoons kirsch. Scatter half the cherries over.

3 Use a swivel-headed potato peeler to grate about 2 tablespoons chocolate from the bar. Set aside ½ for decoration.

4 Melt the rest of the chocolate in a bowl in the microwave or over a pan of simmering water. Then warm the custard through in a bowl in the microwave or a saucepan, for a minute until just warmed, stirring halfway through.

5 Mix just over half the melted chocolate into the custard and beat well. Chill for 10 minutes or longer. Spread the rest of the melted chocolate onto parchment paper on a tray and leave in a cool place (not the fridge) to set firm.

6 Whip the double cream and single cream together with the sugar and vanilla, until just thickened. Spoon about a third of the mixture over the cherries. Add the rest of the cake, broken in halves, spoon over 2 more tablespoons cherry juice and 1 tablespoon of kirsch, then add the rest of the cherries. Spoon the chocolate custard over, then add spoonfuls of cream on top. Sprinkle with the grated chocolate.

7 Cut out star shapes, or other festive shapes, from the set chocolate and use to decorate the trifle just before serving. Chill until ready to serve, if you have time.

TIP

The trifle tastes even better if made in advance so the kirsch can soak into the sponge

Serves 8

Calories: 551

Fat: 18g

Saturated fat: 8g

Suitable for freezing: ✗

- 500g pack luxury vine fruits (mixed dried fruits)
- 300ml (½ pint) dark rum
- Finely grated zest and juice of 1 orange
- 2 teaspoons Angostura bitters
- 4 tablespoons ginger wine
- 60g (2oz) stem ginger, drained from syrup and chopped
- 90g (3oz) molasses sugar
- 30g (1oz) self-raising flour, sieved
- 2 teaspoons ground mixed spice
- 125g (4oz) vegetable suet
- 30g (1oz) flaked almonds
- 90g (3oz) fresh white breadcrumbs
- 1 small carrot, grated
- 2 medium eggs, lightly beaten

TO SERVE:
- 4 pieces of stem ginger, halved
- 8 cocktail cherries
- 8 flaked almonds
- 1 sprig of holly
- 3 tablespoons ginger syrup, from the jar of stem ginger
- 2 tablespoons dark rum

- *1.25 litre (2 pint) pudding basin, baking parchment, string and foil*

Rum and Raisin Christmas Pudding

1 Put the dried fruits into a pan and pour in the rum. Add the orange zest and juice and Angostura bitters. Cover and cook over a medium heat for 5 minutes, just until the rum and fruits are warm. Add the ginger wine and stir in the stem ginger. Pour the dried fruits and liquid into an airtight container and leave overnight to macerate. The following day, pour half of the dried fruit and liquid into a food processor and blend until it is smooth.

2 Crumble the molasses sugar into a large bowl, breaking up any lumps or chunks with your fingertips. Sieve in the flour and mixed spice. Then stir in the suet and almonds

3 Add the blended fruits along with the whole fruits and liquid. Stir in the breadcrumbs and grated carrot, then lastly the eggs. Mix everything together well. Spoon the pudding mixture into the basin. Cover with a double sheet of pleated greaseproof paper and secure with string. Cook in a steamer for 6 hours, checking the pan and topping up with boiling water every 30 minutes or as it needs it.

TO STORE: Cover tightly with fresh baking parchment and foil. Keep in a cool, dark place for up to 3 months.
TO SERVE: Reheat by steaming for 1 hour. Upturn the pudding onto a serving dish. Remove the lining paper on base, top with ginger, cherries and the holly sprig. Drizzle with the ginger syrup.
TO FLAME THE PUDDING: Warm 2 tablespoons of rum in a ladle over a gas flame or microwave it on High for 20 seconds. Pour the warm rum over the pudding and light with a match, standing well back!
TO PRESSURE-COOK THE PUDDING: Put into a 6-litre pressure cooker filled with 2 litres (3½ pints) water. Heat until the valve pops up, reduce heat and cook for 3 hours.

Festive Christmas Ring

Serves 12-18
Calories: 171
Fat: 6g
Saturated fat: 4g
Suitable for freezing: ✔

FOR THE DOUGH:
- 250g (8oz) strong plain flour
- 60g (2oz) caster sugar
- 7g sachet dried fast action yeast
- A pinch of salt
- 6 tablespoons warm milk
- 60g (2oz) butter, melted
- 1 medium egg, beaten
- 30g (1oz) butter, melted

FOR THE FILLING:
- 250g (8oz) dried mixed fruit
- 50g (1¾oz) blanched almonds, chopped
- 50g (1¾oz) caster sugar
- 1 level teaspoon ground mixed spice
- 1 level teaspoon ground cinnamon

FOR THE ICING:
- 6 tablespoons icing sugar

- *Baking sheet, lined with baking parchment*
- *Disposable piping bag*

1 TO MAKE THE DOUGH: Tip the flour into a bowl and add the sugar, yeast and salt. Mix together the milk, butter and egg, then add to the dough and pour into the flour. Mix well, then knead the mixture for about 10 minutes, until it's smooth and elastic.

2 Roll the dough out on a lightly floured surface to a rectangle about 30 x 20cm (12 x 8in). Brush the melted butter over the dough, leaving a 2cm (¾in) area of one of the long edges buttered.

3 TO MAKE THE FILLING: Mix together the dried mixed fruit, chopped almonds, sugar, mixed spice and cinnamon, and spread this out over the buttered area. Brush a line of water along the uncovered edge. Roll the dough up tightly towards the edge with the water, so that the water will seal the dough.

4 Shape the dough into a ring and place it on the lined baking sheet, with the join underneath.

Slash through the dough a number of times, cutting just over halfway through the dough. Cover the dough with a sheet of oiled cling film and leave it in a warm place until it's doubled in size.

5 Set the oven to 200°C or Gas Mark 6. Bake the ring for about 30-45 minutes, or until the ring is golden and sounds hollow underneath. Remove from the oven and slide onto a wire rack to cool.

6 TO MAKE THE ICING: Mix the icing sugar with sufficient water to give a drizzling consistency. Fill the piping bag with the icing and cut off the end of the bag, then pipe lines of icing over the ring. Leave the icing to set before serving.

✳ *Freeze without the icing topping. Wrap well and freeze for up to 1 month. Allow the cake to defrost before piping icing over the top*

Toss-in Fruit Cake

Serves 16-24

Calories: 150

Fat: 5g

Saturated fat: 3g

Suitable for freezing: ✔

- 250g (8oz) self-raising flour
- ½ level teaspoon ground mixed spice
- A pinch of salt
- 125g (4oz) soft brown sugar
- 300-350g (10-12oz) mixed dried fruit
- 60g (2oz) glace cherries, quartered
- 2 medium eggs
- 125ml (4fl oz) oil
- 125ml (4fl oz) milk
- ½ teaspoon almond essence
- 30g (1oz) demerara sugar

- *18cm (7in) square, or 20cm (8in) round cake tin, lined with baking parchment*

1 Set the oven to 150°C or Gas Mark 2. Sift the flour, mixed spice and salt into a mixing bowl. Add the rest of the ingredients, except the demerara sugar. Either beat with a wooden spoon for 3-4 minutes until well mixed, or use an electric mixer and beat for 1-2 minutes. Turn the mixture into the tin and sprinkle with the demerara sugar.

2 Bake just above the centre of the oven for 2 hours, or until a skewer comes out clean after being inserted into the cake. Remove the cake from the oven and leave to cool in the tin.

❈ *Wrap the cold cake in baking parchment, then foil, and freeze for up to 3 months*

Makes 34-36

Calories per pie: 121

Fat per pie: 4.5g

Saturated fat: 3g

Suitable for freezing: ✔

FOR THE PASTRY:
- 250g (8oz) plain flour
- 150g (5oz) cold butter, cubed
- 2 level teaspoons icing sugar
- 1 medium egg yolk
- 650g (1lb 6oz) good mincemeat

FOR THE ICING:
- 125g (4oz) icing sugar
- 1 lemon, zest and
  4 tablespoons juice

- 6.5cm (2¾in) fluted or plain cutter
- Patty tins

Lemon Drizzle Mince Pies

1 Put the flour in a bowl, add the butter and rub it in with your fingertips until it resembles fine breadcrumbs. Stir in the icing sugar, add the egg yolk and 2 tablespoons ice cold water. Stir in with a knife, bring the dough together with your hands and knead lightly to a ball, then flatten to a disc. Wrap in cling film and chill for 30 minutes.

2 Set the oven to 200°C or Gas Mark 6. Roll out half the pastry fairly thinly and cut out rounds. Use to line the tins. Spoon in 1 heaped teaspoon mincemeat.

3 Bake the pies in the oven for 15-18 minutes. When done, take out and put on a wire rack to cool.

Meanwhile, roll out the rest of the pastry and make more mince pies.

4 TO MAKE THE ICING: Sift the icing sugar into a bowl, add the lemon juice and a little water to get a runny icing. Fill a paper or plastic piping bag with the icing and drizzle it over the pies. Sprinkle with lemon zest.

❊ *Freeze pies without icing on. Stack in a plastic container, between sheets of baking parchment. Seal, label and freeze. Use within 3 months. Thaw at room temperature, then drizzle with icing*

TIP

Make the pastry in a food processor if you prefer. If you leave it in the fridge overnight, it will take about an hour to soften before you can roll it out

Sugar and Spice Cookies

Makes about 20

Calories: 135

Fat: 4g

Saturated fat: 1g

Suitable for freezing: ✗

- 2 tablespoons runny honey
- 30g (1oz) unsalted butter
- 60g (2oz) light muscovado sugar
- 250g (8oz) self-raising flour
- 1 teaspoon ground ginger
- ½ teaspoon ground cinnamon
- Finely grated zest of 1 lemon, plus 2-4 tablespoons juice
- 60g (2oz) ground almonds
- 1 large egg

TO DECORATE:
- 50g (5oz) icing sugar, sieved

- *Silver balls*
- *Baking sheets lined with baking parchment*
- *Assorted cookie cutters*
- *Small plain piping nozzle*
- *Piping bag*
- *Ribbon, for hanging, optional*

TIP

These make a perfect Christmas gift, packaged in a tin on a baking tray with some cookie cutters, a small rolling pin and some cookie cutters

1 Put the honey, butter and sugar into a small pan and stir over a low heat until the butter is melted. Sieve the flour, ginger and cinnamon into a bowl. Add the lemon zest and ground almonds.

2 Pour the egg, melted mixture and lemon juice into the dry ingredients. Stir with a wooden spoon until the mixture comes together. Knead the mixture on a lightly floured surface for a couple of minutes, then wrap in cling film and pop in the freezer for 30 minutes to firm up.

3 Set the oven to 180°C or Gas Mark 4. Roll out the dough to a 5mm (¼in) thickness, on a parchment-lined surface, and stamp out the biscuit shapes. Push the tip of a tiny plain piping nozzle near the top edge of each biscuit, and lift out to make a hole if cookies are going to be hung on a tree.

4 Put the cookies onto lined baking sheets. Bake for 15-20 minutes until pale golden. When done, take out and put on a wire rack to cool.

5 TO DECORATE: Mix the icing sugar with 4 teaspoons hot water, to make a smooth icing. Spoon into a paper piping bag with the nozzle. Pipe icing on the biscuits and decorate with silver balls. Leave to set. Thread ribbon through holes, if liked.

Serves 18
Calories: 270
Fat: 8g
Saturated fat: 3.5g
Suitable for freezing: ✔

FOR THE PARKIN:
- 350g (12oz) self-raising flour
- 175g (6oz) light muscovado sugar
- 2 teaspoons ground ginger
- 1 teaspoon mixed spice
- ½ teaspoon baking powder
- 45g (1½oz) coarse or medium oatmeal
- 60g (2oz) pecan nuts, chopped, optional
- 175g (6oz) golden syrup
- 90g (3oz) butter
- 2 medium eggs
- 300ml (½ pint) milk
- 4 stem ginger, finely chopped, to decorate

FOR THE SYRUP:
- 125g (4oz) golden syrup
- 150ml (¼ pint) whisky
- ½ teaspoon mixed spice
- 4 tablespoons stem ginger syrup

- *18 x 28cm (7 x 11in) traybake tin, lined with baking parchment*

Parkin with Whisky Syrup

1 Set the oven to 150°C or Gas Mark 2.
TO MAKE THE PARKIN: Put all the dry ingredients into a large bowl.

2 Melt the syrup with the butter in a pan. Beat the eggs into the milk and add to the dry ingredients with the buttery syrup and beat well. Pour the mixture into the lined traybake tin.

3 Bake for 1 hour 10 minutes until risen and just firm to the touch.

4 TO MAKE THE SYRUP: Warm all the ingredients in a pan. Pierce the hot cake all over and drizzle with half the syrup. Sprinkle with chopped ginger. Serve warm, cut into squares with the extra syrup to pour over.

❋ *Wrap whole cake in a freezer bag and freeze for up to 3 months. Keep syrup in a jar, labelled, in the fridge. Thaw parkin at room temperature. Warm as above and serve with warmed syrup*

Woman's Weekly Cooking Yearbook 2014

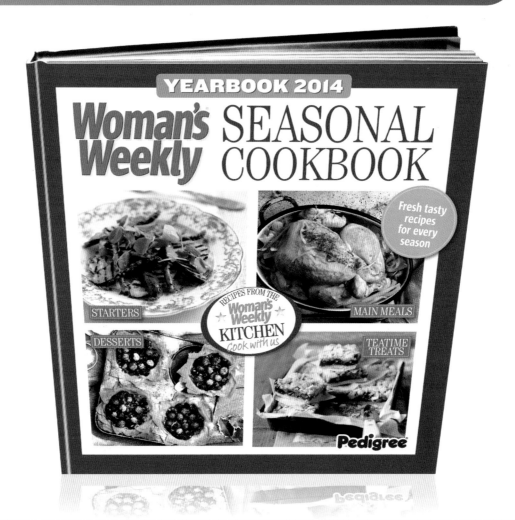

Visit www.pedigreebooks.com

Pedigree Books, Beech Hill House, Walnut Gardens, Exeter EX4 4DH